*Simple
Object-Oriented Design*

Simple
Object-Oriented Design

CREATE CLEAN, MAINTAINABLE APPLICATIONS

MAURÍCIO ANICHE

MANNING

SHELTER ISLAND

For online information and ordering of this and other Manning books, please visit
www.manning.com. The publisher offers discounts on this book when ordered in quantity.
For more information, please contact

Special Sales Department
Manning Publications Co.
20 Baldwin Road
PO Box 761
Shelter Island, NY 11964
Email: orders@manning.com

Manning Publications Co.
20 Baldwin Road
PO Box 761
Shelter Island, NY 11964

Development editor: Toni Arritola
Technical editor: Matthias Noback
Review editor: Isidora Isakov
Production editor: Keri Hales
Copy editor: Tiffany Taylor
Proofreader: Katie Tennant
Technical proofreader: Srihari Sridharan
Typesetter: Gordan Salinovic
Cover designer: Marija Tudor

ISBN 9781633437999
Printed in the United States of America

To Laura, Thomas, Bono, and Duke,
my lovely family/team

brief contents

contents

preface

Why write another book on object-oriented design when so many are out there? This was the question I had to answer for myself before embarking on this project.

We already possess a wealth of knowledge about object-oriented design from the early works of Dave Parnas, Grady Booch's books on UML and object-oriented analysis, and Eric Evans' domain-driven design approach. However, object-oriented design is not merely a pure engineering task; it transcends into art. No prescribed sequence of steps will unfailingly lead us to an optimal design. Instead, object-oriented design demands a creative approach.

This book delves into object-oriented design from two specific angles: how to prevent the complexity of a system from skyrocketing and how to achieve "good-enough" designs.

First, most of a developer's work revolves around maintaining and evolving existing systems. Unfortunately, without due care, every time you make changes to a software system, it becomes more complex, even if it is well designed from the outset. Therefore, this book greatly emphasizes how to combat the natural growth in complexity.

Second, more often than not, you initially have limited knowledge about what you're building. Despite your best efforts, your first design may fall short. However, that's acceptable if you arrive at a good-enough design. The purpose of this book is not to lead you to always achieve the absolute best possible design, but to enable you to create good designs that empower you to build software effectively.

If you are familiar with the existing literature on object-oriented design, you will recognize many of the principles discussed here. Much of my perspective on good modeling has been inspired by existing work. However, I've infused my own flavor into these ideas. I hope even seasoned developers can glean a thing or two from this book.

Happy reading!

acknowledgments

First, I want to thank Dr. Ismar Frango Silveira. Ismar was the teacher of my first-ever formal course on object-oriented design during my undergrad studies back in 2004. The class was an eye-opener for me. Since then, I've been working diligently to sharpen my skills, but his instruction was the foundation. Although it's been a long time since we spoke last, I've never forgotten his contribution to my career.

I would also like to thank Alberto Souza. Besides being one of my best friends in life, Alberto loves good code as much as I do. Despite living one ocean apart, we still find ways to keep in touch not only about life but also about software engineering. Our conversations have always kept me sharp, and many of my thoughts on class design are influenced by his point of view.

I would like to express my gratitude to Toni Arritola, my development editor at Manning. She has been a great partner on this journey, offering numerous valuable suggestions and being an attentive listener. Whenever I was running low in energy, she consistently provided me with a fresh boost. I also must thank Matthias Noback, trainer and consultant at Noback's Office, who was the technical editor for this book. He made many insightful comments that were very helpful. In addition, many thanks go to the behind-the-scenes production staff who helped create this book in its final form.

To all the reviewers—Adail Retamal, Amit Lamba, Brent Honadel, Colin Hastie, Daivid Morgan, Emanuele Origgi, George Onofrei, Gilbert Beveridge, Goetz Heller, Harsh Raval, Helder da Rocha, Iago Sanjurjo Alvarez, Ismail Tapaal, Juan Durillo, Karl van Heijster, Laud Bentil, Marcus Geselle, Mikael Byström, Mustafa Özçetin, Najeeb Arif, Narayanan Jayaratchagan, Nedim Bambur, Nghia To, Nguyen Tran Chau Giang, Oliver Korten, Patrice Maldague, Peter Szabo, Ranjit Sahai, Robert Trausmuth, Sebastian Palma, Sergio Gutierrez, and Victor Durán—thank you. Your suggestions helped make this a better book. A special thank you goes to Paulo Afonso Parreira, Jr., who sent me very helpful, detailed feedback on the manuscript.

Finally, I would like to thank Laura, my wife. She always supports whatever project I decide to start. Without her support, none of this would be possible.

about this book

Simple Object-Oriented Design presents a set of principles that help developers keep the complexity of their designs under control—in other words, keep it simple. The principles can be grouped into six higher-level ideas:

- Small units of code
- Consistent objects
- Proper dependency management
- Good abstractions
- Properly handled infrastructure
- Well modularized

Who should read this book

Simple Object-Oriented Design is a book for software developers who want to sharpen their object-oriented design skills. We discuss code complexity, consistency and encapsulation, dependency management, designing abstractions, handling infrastructure, and modularization in depth. If you are an advanced developer who is familiar with similar approaches, such as clean architecture, you'll still benefit from this book's unique perspective.

Readers must have basic knowledge of object-oriented concepts such as classes, polymorphism, and interfaces. The code examples are written in pseudo-Java code but can be understood by developers familiar with any object-oriented programming language such as C#, Python, or Ruby.

How this book is organized: A road map

This book contains object-oriented design principles derived from my experience. The principles are grouped into six dimensions (complexity, consistency, dependency management, abstractions, infrastructure, and modularization), one per chapter.

Principles are first introduced theoretically and later illustrated with code examples. No new ideas are introduced in the code examples, so more experienced readers can skip them if they wish. You'll also notice that the examples are small in terms of lines of code and complexity. It's impractical to illustrate all the principles in this book with real-world examples from large-scale software systems. Instead, I demonstrate the ideas with small snippets, and it's up to you, the reader, to generalize the idea.

I do my best to provide context, pros and cons, tradeoffs, and when and when not to apply the principles. Nevertheless, as with any best practice, you should consider your context and not blindly adopt what you find here.

Chapters end with a few exercises in which I ask you to discuss the ideas covered in that chapter with a colleague. They are broad and open on purpose. I don't provide answers to these questions because there are no one-size-fits-all responses.

Chapter 1 introduces why systems become complex over time, why we must continuously combat the growth of complexity, and why this endeavor is less painful than it may seem. Then, chapters 2–7 delve into the six higher-level ideas.

Chapter 2 discusses the importance of keeping code simple. In a nutshell, it covers how to break large units of code into smaller pieces, isolate new complexity from existing code units, and document code effectively to improve understanding.

Chapter 3 focuses on maintaining objects' consistency at all times. It explores the problems that arise when objects fall into an inconsistent state and how to implement validation mechanisms that ensure objects remain consistent throughout.

Chapter 4 delves into dependencies and how managing them properly is fundamental for a simple design. It explains how to reduce the effect of coupling in the design, how to model stable classes that are less likely to change, and why dependency injection is crucial for effective dependency management.

Chapter 5 discusses abstractions and how to design them to facilitate software system evolution without altering numerous classes each time.

Chapter 6 concentrates on handling infrastructure code without compromising the design. The chapter explains how to decouple infrastructure code from the domain, allowing changes in one without affecting the other.

Chapter 7 explores modularity: specifically, how to design modules that provide complex features through simple interfaces, how to minimize dependencies among modules, and the importance of defining ownership and engagement rules.

Chapter 8 offers some final advice about the importance of being pragmatic, the necessity for continuous refactoring, and the value of perpetual learning about object-oriented design.

About the code

This book contains many examples of source code both in numbered listings and in line with normal text. In both cases, source code is formatted in a `fixed-width font like this` to separate it from ordinary text.

In many cases, the original source code has been reformatted; we've added line breaks and reworked indentation to accommodate the available page space in the book. Additionally, comments in the source code have often been removed from the listings when the code is described in the text. Code annotations accompany many of the listings, highlighting important concepts.

liveBook discussion forum

Purchase of *Simple Object-Oriented Design* includes free access to live-Book, Manning's online reading platform. Using liveBook's exclusive discussion features, you can attach comments to the book globally or to specific sections or paragraphs. It's a snap to make notes for yourself, ask and answer technical questions, and receive help from the author and other users. To access the forum, go to https://livebook .manning.com/book/simple-object-oriented-design/discussion. You can also learn more about Manning's forums and the rules of conduct at https://livebook.manning.com/discussion.

Manning's commitment to our readers is to provide a venue where a meaningful dialogue between individual readers and between readers and the author can take place. It is not a commitment to any specific amount of participation on the part of the author, whose contribution to the forum remains voluntary (and unpaid). We suggest you try asking him some challenging questions lest his interest stray! The forum and the archives of previous discussions will be accessible from the publisher's website as long as the book is in print.

Other online resources

If you want to continue reading my thoughts on object-oriented design and software testing, subscribe to my newsletter: https:// effectivesoftwaretesting.substack.com.

about the author

MAURÍCIO ANICHE'S mission is to help software engineers become better and more productive. Maurício is currently a Tech Lead at Adyen, where he leads different engineering enablement initiatives, including Adyen's Tech Academy, a team focused on additional training and education for engineers. Maurício is also an assistant professor of software engineering at Delft University of Technology in the Netherlands. His teaching efforts in software testing earned him the Computer Science Teacher of the Year 2021 award and the TU Delft Education Fellowship, a prestigious fellowship given to innovative lecturers. He is the author of *Effective Software Testing: A Developer's Guide* (Manning, 2022).

about the cover illustration

The figure on the cover of *Simple Object-Oriented Design* is "Femme de l'Isle Scio," or "Woman of Chios Island," taken from a collection by Jacques Grasset de Saint-Sauveur, published in 1788. Each illustration is finely drawn and colored by hand.

In those days, it was easy to identify where people lived and what their trade or station in life was just by their dress. Manning celebrates the inventiveness and initiative of the computer business with book covers based on the rich diversity of regional culture centuries ago, brought back to life by pictures from collections such as this one.

It's all about
managing complexity

This chapter covers
- Why software systems get more complex over time
- The challenges of object-oriented design
- Why we should keep improving our design over time

In 2010, I worked for a great internet company as part of a team responsible for billing. The company founder wrote the first version of the system 10 or 15 years before I joined. The logic was all in complex SQL Server stored procedures, each of which had thousands of lines of code. It was time to refactor this existing billing infrastructure into something new, and I can't count the number of hours we spent talking to the financial team so that we could create a design that would fit all their current and future needs.

1

The great news is that we made it. With our new implementation, we could add new products or financial rules in hours. The financial team was very happy with us. Feature requests that in the past took weeks now took a couple of days. The quality was also much higher. Our design was highly testable, so we rarely introduced regression bugs. Even our most junior engineer could easily navigate the code and feel confident enough to make critical changes. In a word, our new design was *simple*.

I've been developing object-oriented software systems for 20 years and have learned that in an object-oriented system without a proper design, even simple things are too hard. It doesn't have to be like this.

1.1   *Object-oriented design and the test of time*

Object-oriented programming is always a great choice when implementing complex software systems where flexibility and maintainability are requisites. However, solely picking an object-oriented language for your project isn't enough. You need to make good use of it.

Luckily, we don't have to invent best practices for object-oriented systems from scratch, as our community already has extensive knowledge. If you don't know much about existing best practices or want to revisit them, this book is perfect for you, and you should read it cover to cover, including the code examples. If you are already a more senior engineer and aware of the existing best practices, this book will give you a different and pragmatic view of them, which will hopefully trigger interesting discussions in your mind.

Here are some common questions that emerge when almost any developer is building an information system using an object-oriented language:

- Is this implementation simple enough, or should I propose a more elegant abstraction?
- This class goes through many states during its life cycle. How can I ensure that it's always in a consistent state?
- How should I model the interaction between my system and an external web app?
- Is it okay to make this class depend on this other class, or is that coupling bad?

This book is called *Simple Object-Oriented Design* because *simple object-oriented designs are always easier to maintain.* The challenge is not only to develop a simple design but also to keep it that way. I learned a lot from my good and bad decisions over the years, and that's what I'll share in this book: the set of patterns that help me deliver object-oriented software systems that are easy to maintain and evolve.

1.2 *Designing simple object-oriented systems*

"As software systems evolve, their complexity increases unless work is done to maintain or reduce it."

This insight comes from Manny Lehman's 1984 paper, "On understanding laws, evolution, and conservation in the large-program life cycle" (https://dl.acm.org/doi/10.1016/0164-1212%2879%2990022-0). Evolving software systems of any type isn't straightforward. We know that code tends to decay over time and requires effort to maintain. And despite 40 years of progress, the maintainability of software systems remains a challenge.

In essence, maintainability is the effort you put into completing tasks like modifying business rules, adding features, identifying bugs, and patching the system. Highly maintainable software enables developers to perform such tasks with reasonable effort, whereas low maintainability makes tasks too difficult, time consuming, and bug prone.

Many factors affect maintainability, from overly complex code to dependency management, poorly designed abstractions, and bad modularization. Systems naturally become more complex over time, so continually adding code without considering its consequences for maintenance can quickly lead to a messy codebase.

Consistently combating complexity growth is crucial, even if it seems time consuming. And I know it's more effort than simply "dumping code." But trust me, developers feel much worse when handling big balls of mud the entire day. You may have worked on codebases that were hard to maintain. I did. Doing anything in such systems takes a lot of time. You can't find where to write your code, all the code you write feels like it's a workaround, you can't write automated tests because the code is untestable, you are always afraid something will go wrong because you never feel confident about changing the code, and so on.

What constitutes a simple object-oriented design? Based on my experience, it's a design that presents the following six characteristics, also illustrated in figure 1.1:

- Simple code
- Consistent objects
- Proper dependency management
- Good abstractions
- Properly handled external dependencies and infrastructure
- Well modularized

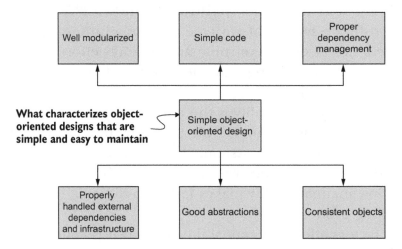

Figure 1.1   Characteristics of a simple object-oriented design

These ideas may sound familiar to you. They are all popular in object-oriented systems. Let's look at what I mean by each of them and what happens when we lose control, all in a nutshell.

1.2.1   *Simple code*

Implementing methods and classes that are simple is a great way to start your journey toward maintainable object-oriented design. Consider a method that began as a few lines with a handful of conditional statements but grew over time and now has hundreds of lines and `if`s inside of `if`s. Maintaining such a method is tricky.

Interestingly, classes and methods usually start simple and manageable. But if we don't work to keep them like this, they become hard to understand and maintain, as in figure 1.2. Complex code tends to result in bugs, which are drawn to complex implementations that are difficult to understand. Complex code is also challenging to maintain, refactor, and test, as developers fear breaking something and struggle to identify all possible test cases.

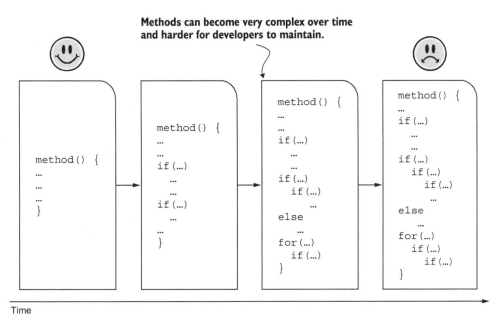

Figure 1.2   Simple code becomes complex over time and, consequently, very hard to maintain.

There are many ways to reduce the complexity of a class or method. For example, clear and expressive variable names help developers better understand what's going on. However, in this part of the book, I argue that the number-one rule to keep classes and methods simple is to keep them *small*. A method shouldn't be too long. A class shouldn't have too many methods. Smaller units of code are always easier to maintain and evolve.

1.2.2   *Consistent objects*

It's much easier to work on a system when you can trust that objects are always in a consistent state and any attempt to make them inconsistent is denied. When consistency isn't accounted for in the design, objects may hold invalid states, leading to bugs and maintainability problems.

Consider a `Basket` class in an e-commerce system that tracks the products a person is buying and their final value. The total value must be updated whenever we add a product to or remove a product from the basket. The basket should also reject invalid client requests, like adding a product more than one time or removing a product that isn't in the basket.

In figure 1.3, the left side shows a protected basket: items can only be added or removed by asking the basket to do so. The basket is in complete control and ensures its consistency. On the right side, the unprotected basket allows unrestricted access to its contents. Given the lack of control, that basket can't always ensure consistency.

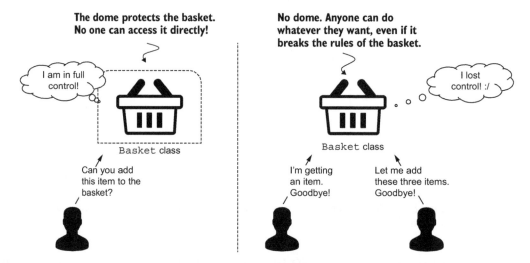

Figure 1.3   Two baskets: one that has control over the actions that happen on it and another that doesn't. Managing state and consistency is fundamental.

We'll see that a good design ensures that objects can't ever be in an inconsistent state. Consistency can be mishandled in many ways, such as improper setter methods that bypass consistency checks or a lack of flexible validation mechanisms, which we'll discuss in more detail later.

1.2.3   *Proper dependency management*

In large-scale object-oriented systems, dependency management becomes critical to maintainability. In a system where the coupling is high and no one cares which classes are coupled to which other classes, any simple change may have unpredicted consequences.

Figure 1.4 shows how the Basket class may be affected by changes in any of its dependencies: DiscountRules, Product, and Customer. Even a change in DiscountRepository, a transitive dependency, may affect Basket. For example, if the Product class changes frequently, Basket is always at risk of having to change as well.

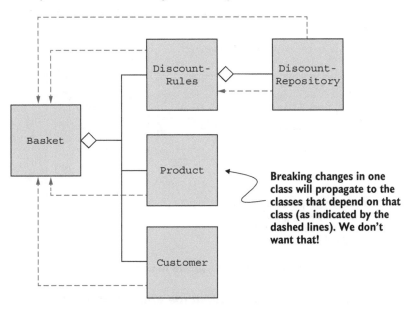

Figure 1.4   Dependency management and change propagation

Simple object-oriented designs aim to minimize dependencies among classes. The less they depend on each other and the less they know about each other, the better. Good dependency management also ensures that classes depend as much as possible on stable components that are less likely to change and, therefore, less likely to provoke cascading changes.

1.2.4   *Good abstractions*

Simple code is always preferred, but it may not be sufficient for extensibility. Extending a class by adding more code stops being effective at some point and becomes a burden.

Imagine implementing 30 or 40 different business rules in the same class or method. I illustrate that in figure 1.5. Note how the `DiscountRules` class, a class that's responsible for applying different discounts in our e-commerce system, grows as new discount rules are introduced, making the class much harder to maintain. A good design provides developers with abstractions that help them evolve the system without making existing classes more complex.

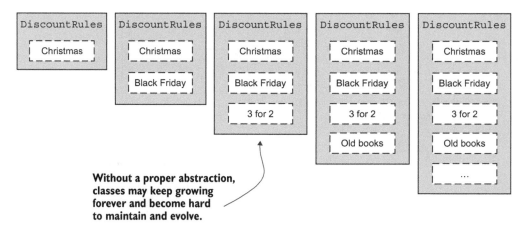

Figure 1.5   A class that has no abstractions grows in complexity indefinitely.

1.2.5   *Properly handled external dependencies and infrastructure*

Simple object-oriented designs separate domain code that contains business logic from code required for communication with external dependencies. Figure 1.6 shows domain classes on the left and the classes that handle communication with other systems and infrastructure on the right.

Letting infrastructure details leak into your domain code may hinder your ability to make changes in the infrastructure. Imagine that all the code to access the database is spread through the codebase. Now you must add a caching layer to speed up the application's response time. You may have to change the code everywhere for that to happen.

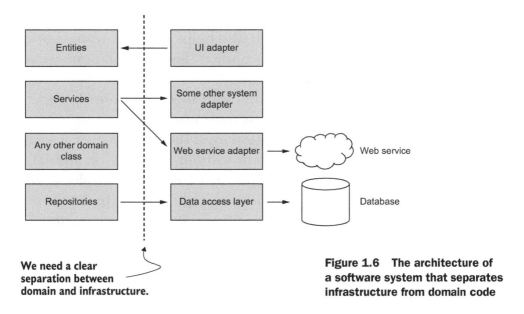

We need a clear separation between domain and infrastructure.

Figure 1.6 The architecture of a software system that separates infrastructure from domain code

The challenge lies in abstracting irrelevant or external aspects of your infrastructure while using valuable features provided by the infrastructure. For instance, if you are using a relational database like Postgres, you may want to hide its presence from the domain code but still be able to use its unique features that enhance productivity or performance.

Why do you call it infrastructure?

I use the term *infrastructure* to refer to any dependency on external systems and resources such as web services, databases, third-party APIs, and anything beyond your system's border. Whenever you have such a dependency, you must write code connecting your system to the external system or resource. We'll focus on writing this "glue code" flexibly so it doesn't harm the rest of your design in chapter 6.

1.2.6 *Well modularized*

As software systems grow, fitting everything into a single component or module is challenging. Simple object-oriented designs divide large systems into independent components that interact to achieve a common goal.

Dividing systems into smaller components makes them easier to maintain and understand. It also helps different teams work on separate components without conflicts. Smaller components are more manageable and testable.

Consider a software system with three domains: Invoice, Billing, and Delivery. These domains must work together, with Invoice and Delivery requiring information from Billing.

Figure 1.7 shows a system without modules on the left, where classes from different domains mix freely. As complexity increases, this becomes unmanageable. The right side of the figure shows the same system divided into modules: Billing, Invoice, and Delivery. Modules interact through interfaces, ensuring that clients use only what's needed without understanding the entire domain.

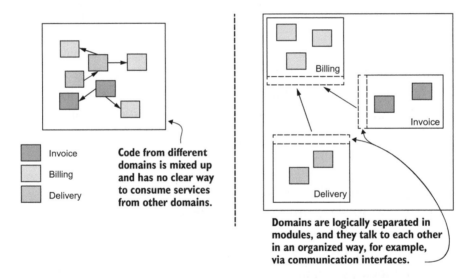

Figure 1.7   Two software systems with different modularization approaches

It's not easy to identify the right level of granularity for a module or what its public interface should look like. We'll discuss this later.

1.3   *Simple design as a day-to-day activity*

As I said, creating a simple design isn't usually a complex challenge, but keeping it simple as the system evolves is. We must keep improving and simplifying our designs as we learn more about the system. For that to happen, we must transform design into an everyday activity.

1.3.1   *Reducing complexity is similar to personal hygiene*

Constantly working toward simplifying the design can be compared to brushing your teeth. Although not particularly exciting, it's necessary to avoid discomfort and costly problems in the future. Similarly, investing a little time in code maintenance daily helps prevent more significant problems down the line.

1.3.2   *Complexity may be necessary but should not be permanent*

Sometimes a degree of complexity is needed to uncover a simpler and more elegant solution to a problem. Many believe complexity can't be sidestepped. Starting with a complex solution isn't a problem; the problem lies in maintaining complexity indefinitely. Once you identify a simpler solution, it's time to plan for refactoring.

1.3.3   *Consistently addressing complexity is cost effective*

Regularly addressing complexity keeps both the time and cost associated with it within reasonable limits. Delaying complexity management can result in significantly higher expenses and make refactoring more difficult and time consuming.

The *technical debt* metaphor helps us understand this. Coined by Ward Cunningham, the idea is to see coding problems as financial debt. The additional effort required for maintenance due to past poor decisions represents interest on this debt. This concept relates closely to this book's focus; complexity escalates if code structure isn't improved, leading to excessive interest payments.

I've seen codebases where everyone knew that parts of them were very complex and challenging to maintain, but no one dared to refactor them. Trust me, you don't want to get there.

1.3.4   *High-quality code promotes good practices*

When developers work with well-structured code with proper abstractions, straightforward methods, and comprehensive tests, they are more likely to maintain the code's quality. Conversely, messy code often leads to further disorganization and degradation in quality. This concept is similar to the broken-window theory, which explains how maintaining orderly environments can prevent further disorder.

1.3.5   *Controlling complexity isn't as difficult as it seems*

The key to ensuring that complexity doesn't grow out of hand is recognizing the signs as soon as possible and addressing them early. With experience and knowledge, developers can detect and resolve most problems in the initial stages of development. Problems that are detected and tackled early enough are cheaper and faster to fix.

1.3.6   *Keeping the design simple is a developer's responsibility*

Creating high-quality software systems that are easy to evolve and maintain can be challenging but is necessary. As developers, managing complexity is part of our job and contributes to more efficient and sustainable software systems.

Striking the right balance between manageable complexity and overwhelming chaos is challenging. Starting with complex abstractions may prevent problems, but it adds system complexity. A more straightforward method with two `if` statements is easier to understand than a convoluted interface. On the other hand, at some point, simple code is no longer enough. Striving for extensibility in every piece of code would create chaos. It's our job to find the right balance between simplicity and complexity.

1.3.7   *Good-enough designs*

In the book *A Philosophy of Software Design* (https://web.stanford .edu/~ouster/cgi-bin/book.php), John Ousterhout says it takes him at least three rewrites to get to the best design for a given problem. I couldn't agree more.

Often, the most effective designs emerge after several iterations. In many cases, it's more practical to focus on creating "good-enough designs" that are easily understood, maintained, and evolved rather than strive for perfection from the outset. Again, the key is to identify when simple is no longer good enough.

1.4   *A short dive into the architecture of an information system*

Let me define a few terms before discussing different patterns to help you keep your design simple. We can examine object-oriented design from many different angles. If you are building a framework that's supposed to be highly generic, you may have different concerns than someone developing an enterprise system. In this book, I focus on object-oriented design for information or enterprise systems. An information system helps us organize information. Think of the back office of an online store, a financial system that processes payments and customer billing, or an e-learning system that handles all the students at a university.

Figure 1.8 illustrates what usually happens behind an information system. These systems are often characterized as having the following:

- A frontend that displays all the information to the user. This frontend is often implemented as a web page. Developers can use many technologies to build modern frontends, such as React, Angular, VueJS, or even plain vanilla JavaScript, CSS, and HTML. In this book, we focus not on the design of the frontend but rather on the backend.
- A backend that handles requests from the frontend. The backend is where most, if not all, business logic lives. The backend may communicate with other software systems, such as external or internal web services, to achieve its tasks.
- A database that stores all the information. Backend systems are strongly database centric. This means most backend actions involve retrieving, inserting, updating, or deleting information from the database.

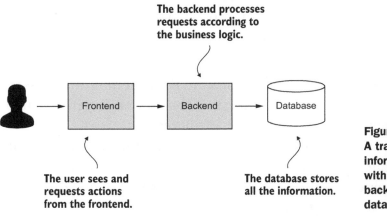

The backend processes requests according to the business logic.

The user sees and requests actions from the frontend.

The database stores all the information.

**Figure 1.8
A traditional information system with a frontend, a backend, and a database**

Let me also define the inside of a backend system and a few terms (see figure 1.9). A backend system receives requests via any protocol (usually HTTP) from any other system: for example, a traditional web-based frontend. Today, we commonly use a Model-View-Controller (MVC) framework to help us build the application.

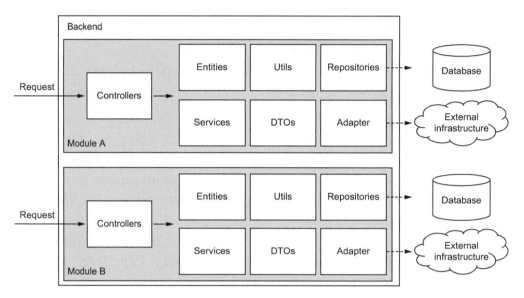

Figure 1.9   The internal design of a backend system

A Controller first receives the user request. The Controller's primary responsibility is to convert the user request into a series of commands to the domain Model that knows the business rules. The domain Model is composed of different types of classes. This depends on the architectural patterns your application is following, but you often see the following:

- *Entities* model business concepts. Think of an `Invoice` class that models what invoices mean to the system. Entity classes contain attributes that describe the concept and methods that consistently manipulate these attributes.
- *Services* encapsulate more complex business rules that involve one or more entities. Think of a `GenerateInvoice` service that generates the final invoice for a user who decides to pay for all the products in their basket.

- *Repositories* contain all the logic to retrieve and persist information. Behind the scenes, their implementation talks to a database.
- *Data-transfer objects* (DTOs) are classes that hold information and transfer information from different layers.
- *Utility classes* contain a set of utility methods not offered by your programming language or framework of choice.

Backends also commonly have to communicate with other external applications, usually via remote calls or specific protocols. Think of a web service that enables the application to send a request to a governmental system, or a Simple Mail Transfer Protocol (SMTP) server that enables the application to send e-mails. Anything that's outside and somewhat out of the control of the backend, I call *infrastructure.*

A large-scale backend may also be organized in modules. Each module contains its domain Model with entities, repositories, services, etc. Modules may also send messages to each other.

If you're familiar with architectural patterns such as Clean Architecture, Hexagonal Architecture, Domain-Driven Design, or any other layered architecture, you may have opinions about how things should be organized. The diagram in figure 1.9 is meant to be generic enough that anyone can fit it into their favorite architecture.

The figure also shows the two modules inside the same backend, which may lead you to think I'm proposing monoliths over a service-distributed architecture. Again, this figure is meant to be generic. Different modules can live in the same distributed binary and communicate via simple method calls or distributed over the network and communicate via remote procedure calls. It doesn't matter at this point.

1.5   The example project: PeopleGrow!

To illustrate the design patterns throughout the book, I use an imaginary backend system called PeopleGrow!, illustrated in figure 1.10. It's an information system that manages employees and their growth through training courses.

The system handles different features, some of which are highlighted here. The italicized domain terms appear frequently in the following chapters:

- The list of *trainings* and *learning paths* (collections of trainings).
- The *employees* and the training courses that they took or still have to take.
- Training courses are offered multiple times each year. Each *offering* contains the training course's date and the maximum number of participants allowed.
- Participants can *enroll* in the offerings themselves or be enrolled by the administrator.
- The training courses and the *trainers* who deliver them.
- All sorts of *reports*, such as which training courses don't have an instructor assigned, which training courses are full, etc.
- Convenient functionality such as calendar invites through the company's calendar system, automatic messages via the company's internal chat, and e-mail notifications.
- A frontend available for *administrators* to add new training courses and learning paths and see reports.
- Various APIs for any internal system to use. For example, employees can enroll in courses via the company's internal wiki, which uses PeopleGrow!'s APIs.

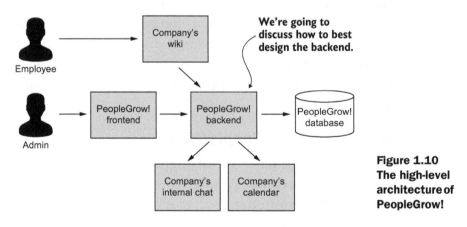

**Figure 1.10
The high-level
architecture of
PeopleGrow!**

Architecturally speaking, PeopleGrow! comprises a frontend, a backend, and a database. As I said, it also can connect to external company systems, such as the internal chat and the calendar system. PeopleGrow!'s API may also be consumed by other company applications, such as its internal wiki.

The backend is implemented using object-oriented languages like Java, C#, and Python. It uses current frameworks for web development and database access. For example, think of Spring Boot and Java Persistence API (JPA) if you are a Java developer; ASP.NET Core MVC and Entity Framework if you are a C# developer; or Django if you are a Python developer. Internally, the backend models the business. In the following chapters, I'll write Java-like pseudocode to illustrate the principles, but these are easily understandable by developers familiar with any language.

The team that's building PeopleGrow! is now facing maintenance challenges. Bugs are emerging. Any changes requested by the product team take days to complete. Developers are always afraid of making changes, and an innocent change often affects unexpected areas of the system. Let's dive into the design decisions of PeopleGrow! and improve them!

1.6 *Exercises*

Think through the following questions or discuss them with a colleague:

1 In your opinion, what constitutes a simple object-oriented design? What's the difference between your point of view and that presented in this chapter?

2 What types of object-oriented design problems have you faced as a developer? What were their consequences? Do they fit in any of the six categories presented in this chapter?

3 Is it possible to keep the design simple as the system evolves? What are the main challenges in keeping it simple?

Summary

- Building a highly maintainable software system requires a good object-oriented design. Simplicity is the key factor for a highly maintainable software system.

- Building simple object-oriented designs is often straightforward, but it's hard to keep the design simple as the complexity of the business grows. Managing complexity is essential to maintain and develop software systems effectively.

- Simple and maintainable object-oriented designs have six characteristics: simple code, consistent objects, proper dependency management, good abstractions, adequately handled infrastructure, and good modularization.

- Managing complexity and keeping designs simple is a continuous process requiring daily attention, like brushing your teeth.

- Writing good code is easier when the existing code is already good. Productivity increases, developers feel confident modifying the code, and business value is delivered faster.

Making code small 2

This chapter covers

- Breaking large units of code into smaller pieces
- Moving new complexity away from existing units of code
- Documenting your code to improve understanding

Complex code is harder to read and understand than simple code. As a developer, you've likely experienced the mental strain of deciphering a 200-line method compared to a 20-line method. You feel tired even before you begin to read it. Highly complex code is also more prone to bugs. It's easier to make mistakes in code that's difficult to grasp. It's also hard to write tests for complex code, as it has too many possibilities and corner cases to explore, and it's too easy to forget one of them.

Making code simple and small is the first thing you should always consider. Even with a well-designed software system, it's easy to lose sight of code complexity. Lines of code tend to become overgrown if we don't actively work to prevent it, leading

19

to oversized classes. Long classes and methods happen more often and more naturally than we like to admit. It's too easy to open an existing class in the system and add more code instead of reflecting on the impact of these new lines and redesigning the code.

The gist of this chapter is that small code is easier to maintain. In the following sections, I'll dive into patterns to help you make your code small.

2.1   *Make units of code small*

> *Classes and methods should be small. That improves code readability, maintainability, and reusability and reduces the likelihood of bugs.*

Business rules in information systems keep evolving and increasing in complexity. The popular quick-and-dirty way to evolve a business rule is to add code to methods and classes: either adding lines of code to an existing method or adding methods to existing classes. Suddenly you have a long class, and maintaining it requires a lot of energy from an engineer.

No matter how well crafted a 2,000-line method or class is, it remains challenging to understand. Such methods do too much for any developer, regardless of seniority, to quickly grasp. This may seem like a basic pattern, but trust me, the primary strategy for reducing code complexity is to decrease the unit's size. It's that simple.

Developers sometimes debate whether having more classes is a drawback. Some argue that it's easier to follow code if it's all in the same file. Although software design has tradeoffs, academic studies like the 2012 paper "An Exploratory Study of the Impact of Antipatterns on class Change- and Fault-Proneness" by Khomh and colleagues shows that longer methods are more susceptible to changes and defects.

It doesn't take much to convince someone that breaking complex code into smaller units is a good approach. Smaller units are always better than oversized units.

First, small classes or units of code allow developers to read less. If the implementation is visible, they will likely read it whether they need to or not. But if a method calls another class, they'll only open that code when needed. Although some argue that navigation becomes trickier when jumping between classes, modern IDEs make navigation easy when you master it.

Second, small units of code enable extensibility from day one. Refactoring complex behavior into smaller classes often involves seeing the code as a set of pieces that, together, form a puzzle. Once modeled, each piece can be replaced if needed.

Finally, testability improves: smaller classes let developers decide whether to write isolated unit tests for specific parts of the business logic. Sometimes we want to exercise one piece in isolation and other times all the pieces together. You don't have that choice if the behavior is all in one place.

In practice, we should build complex behavior using smaller methods or classes, as illustrated in figure 2.1. The classes and methods shown are all small and do only one thing. Anyone can easily understand the code, and testing is easy.

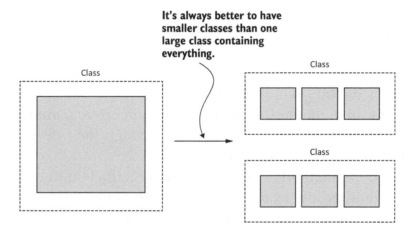

Figure 2.1   Smaller units are always better than large units.

In the following subsections, I discuss a few heuristics of when to break code into methods and classes. We also discuss the exceptional cases where you don't want to break code into small units.

2.1.1   *Break complex methods into private methods*

Breaking a large method into a few smaller ones is an excellent and easy way to reduce complexity. All you need to do is identify a piece of code within a large method that can be moved to a private method.

What does "cohesion" mean?

A *cohesive* component (class or method) has a single, clear responsibility within the system—it does only one thing. A class that does one thing is undoubtedly smaller than a class that does multiple things. If we strive for cohesive code, we naturally strive for simple code.

Private methods

Private methods can only be called from within the same class they're declared in. They're a perfect solution when you want to isolate a piece of code from the rest but don't want it to be visible and possibly called from outside the class.

An excellent way to determine whether a new private method makes sense or whether a code segment can be an independent unit is by evaluating the following:

- Can you assign a clear name to the private method that explains its purpose?
- Does the new method perform a cohesive, small action that the public method can easily use?
- Is the new method dependent on numerous parameters or class dependencies, or is it concise enough for a developer to understand its requirements quickly?
- When the method is called, is its name sufficient to explain its function without examining the implementation?
- Could this private method be made static? Such methods often make good candidates for extraction, as they don't rely on the original class. I don't want you to make the method static, but this is a nice trick to see if the method is independent.

How do you test a private method?

A test method can't invoke private methods. After all, they are private. A private method should be tested through the public method that calls it. If you feel the urge to unit-test that private method in isolation, consider moving the code to another class, as I explain next.

2.1.2   Move a complex unit of code to another class

Private methods may not be the ideal location for extracted code, particularly if it's unrelated to the main goal of the large unit. Consider the following to decide whether to move code to another class instead of a private method:

- Does this piece of code do something different than the rest of the class?
- Does it do something important enough for the domain that it deserves its own name and class?
- Do you want to test this piece of code in isolation?
- Does this code depend on classes you don't want the rest of the code to depend on?
- Is it too big to break into many other private methods?

Believe it or not, one of the most significant challenges in moving behavior to a new class is naming the new class. If you can quickly come up with a good name and know precisely which package this class should live in, then you should do it.

2.1.3   When not to divide code into small units

Every rule has exceptions. When should code be kept together?

- When two or more puzzle pieces can't live apart. Forcing separation often results in complex method signatures.
- When a puzzle piece is unlikely to be replaced.
- When there's little value in testing a part in complete isolation.
- When there are few puzzle pieces. If you only need two to four private methods, why complicate your code?

As always, pragmatism is critical.

> ### Be careful about classitis
> In the insightful book *A Philosophy of Software Design*, John Ousterhout argues that having too many small classes can hinder maintainability. He refers to creating too many small classes as *classitis*. He has a point. You don't want micro classes, just as you don't want huge blocks of code.

2.1.4   *Get a helicopter view of the refactoring before you do it*

In more complex refactorings, I try to picture what the final code will look like once I'm done:

- What will the classes look like after the refactoring, and how will they relate to each other?
- Do I like what I see?
- Do I see any design issues?

I don't do this in a formal way. If I can't see the final result in my mind, I draw diagrams on a piece of paper or whiteboard, usually in a Unified Modeling Language (UML)-like form.

2.1.5   *Example: Importing employees*

Employees are imported into PeopleGrow! in batches. The administrator uploads a comma-separated values (CSV) file containing each employee's name, email, role, and starting date. If the employee is already in the database, PeopleGrow! updates their information.

The initial implementation looked like what you see in listing 2.1. The code parses the CSV using a third-party library. Then, for each employee in the import data, the system either creates a new employee or updates an existing one in the database.

Although the code isn't complicated, remember that this is just an illustration. The importing service could have hundreds of lines in a real software system.

> **Listing 2.1   A large method that should be broken down**

```
class ImportEmployeesService {

  private EmployeeRepository employees;

  public ImportEmployeesService(EmployeeRepository employees) {
    this.employees = employees;
  }

  public ImportResult import(String csv) {

    var result = new ImportResult();

    var csvParser = new CsvParserLibrary();
    csvParser.setMode(CsvParserLibrary.Mode.IGNORE_ERRORS);
    csvParser.setObjectType(EmployeeParsedData.class);
    List<EmployeeParsedData> importedList =
      csvParser.parse(csv);
```

Parses the CSV using the fictitious CsvParserLibrary

```
for(var employee in importedList) {              ┐ Looks for an existing
    var maybeAnEmployee =                        │ employee in the DB
        employees.findByEmail(employee.email()); ◄─┘ by their email
    if(maybeAnEmployee.isEmpty()) {          ◄────┐
        var newEmployee = new Employee(          │
            employee.getName(),              ┐ If the employee doesn't
            employee.getEmail(),             │ exist, creates a new one
            employee.getStartingDate(),
            employee.getRole());

        employees.save(newEmployee);              ┐ If the employee already
        result.addedNewEmployee(newEmployee);     │ exists, updates their
                                           ◄──────┘ information
    } else {
        var currentEmployee = maybeAnEmployee.get();
        currentEmployee.setName(name);
        currentEmployee.setStartingDate(startingDate);
        currentEmployee.setRole(role);

        employees.update(currentEmployee);
        result.updatedEmployee(currentEmployee);
    }
}

    return result;
  }
}

record EmployeeParsedData(
    String name,
    String email,
    LocalDate startingDate,     ┐ Data structure to store the
    String role) { }        ◄───┘ data that comes from the CSV
```

The import method does too much. It's easy to get lost in the code. Let's reduce its complexity by moving code away from it. First, let's move the CSV-parsing logic to another class. Even though these few lines of code only delegate the real work to the CsvParserLibrary class, it's a different responsibility and will look good in its own class.

NOTE   In future chapters, I'll also discuss wrapping up calls to third-party libraries—which is also, in general, a good idea.

The EmployeeImportCSVParser class offers a parse method that returns a list of EmployeeParsedData. The implementation is the same as before.

Listing 2.2   CSV parser in its own class

```
class EmployeeImportCSVParser {

  public List<EmployeeParsedData> parse(String csv) {        ◁─────┐  The parsing
    var csvParser = new CsvParserLibrary();                          algorithm is now
    csvParser.setMode(CsvParserLibrary.Mode.IGNORE_ERRORS);         in the parse()
    csvParser.setObjectType(EmployeeParsedData.class);              method.
    return csvParser.parse(csv);
  }

}
```

There's still more we can do in ImportEmployeesService. We can make
the import method only control the flow and let other classes or
methods implement the actions. For example, the two blocks of
code in the if statement—one that creates a new employee and
another that updates them—can be extracted to a private method.

I don't envision these two methods going to different classes.
They seem related, and leaving them in ImportEmployeesService looks
fine for now. I may change my mind in the future, but I like to take
simpler and smaller steps first.

In listing 2.3, the class is much smaller, and the methods are more
cohesive. The import method only coordinates the task. It calls the
new EmployeeImportCSVParser, gets the parsed results, calls Employee-
Repository to see whether the employee is already in the database,
and, based on that, decides which action to take, with each action in
a separate private method.

Listing 2.3   Much smaller ImportEmployeesService

```
class ImportEmployeesService {

  private EmployeeRepository employees;              EmployeeImportCSVParser
  private EmployeeImportCSVParser parser;            is now injected through
                                                      the constructor.
  public ImportEmployeesService(EmployeeRepository employees,
    EmployeeImportCSVParser parser) {        ◁────────────────┘
    this.employees = employees;
    this.parser = parser;
  }

  public ImportResult import(String csv) {

    var result = new ImportResult();                  Calls the parser class and
                                                      gets the parsing results
    var importedEmployees = parser.parse(csv);   ◁────┘
```

```
  for(var importedEmployee : importedEmployees) {
    var maybeAnEmployee =
    å
employees.findByEmail(importedEmployee.getEmail());

    if(maybeAnEmployee.isEmpty()) {
      createNewEmployee(importedEmployee, result);
    } else {
      updateEmployee(importedEmployee, maybeAnEmployee.get(), result);
    }
  }

  return result;
}

private void createNewEmployee(
  EmployeeParsedData importedEmployee,
  ImportResult result) {

  var newEmployee = new Employee(
    importedEmployee.getName(),
    importedEmployee.getEmail(),
    importedEmployee.getStartingDate(),
    importedEmployee.getRole());

  employees.save(newEmployee);
  result.addedNewEmployee(newEmployee);
}

private void updateEmployee(
  EmployeeParsedData importedEmployee,
  Employee currentEmployee,
  ImportResult result) {
  currentEmployee.setName(name);
  currentEmployee.setStartingDate(startingDate);
  currentEmployee.setRole(role);

  employees.update(currentEmployee);
  result.updatedEmployee(currentEmployee);
}
}
```

Looks for the employee in the database

The if block decides which private method to call.

The logic to create a new employee is moved to this private method.

Same for the logic to update an employee, which is now in a private method.

It takes less time for a developer to read this class and figure out what it does. It also takes less time for a developer to understand each small block. Having methods that focus on the "what" and letting other methods implement the "how" is a good practice that I'll discuss in chapter 5.

ImportEmployeesService now requires EmployeeRepository and EmployeeImportCSVParser in its constructor. This means some other part of the code should instantiate these classes. Receiving dependencies via a constructor is a good idea. We'll discuss dependency injection and dependency management further in general in chapter 4.

> **Good-enough design**
>
> I don't really like that we have to pass `ImportResult` to the private methods. Not bad, but also not elegant. There are other ways to design this. For example, each method could return its own `ImportResult` back to the `import` method, which would merge them all. That would require more code. I don't see the need to overcomplicate this now, so we'll settle for the "good-enough design," as discussed in chapter 1.

Good job. `ImportEmployeesService` is much better now!

2.2   *Make code readable and documented*

Improve the readability of the code, and document it when necessary to minimize the time developers spend trying to understand its purpose and functionality.

Consider how much time you've spent reading code to fix bugs or implement new features in unfamiliar areas. In the book *Clean Code* (Pearson, 2008), Robert Martin estimates that the ratio of time spent reading code to writing code is about 10 to 1. Academic research indicates that programmers spend around 60% of their time reading code (see the 2017 paper, "Measuring Program Comprehension: A Large-Scale Field Study with Professionals," by Xin Xia and colleagues). The less time developers spend reading code, the more productive they become.

Your goal should be to write code that others can easily understand. There are many different patterns and principles that you can apply. *Clean Code* is the canonical reference for writing readable code.

This section focuses on three techniques that increase code legibility and that we should be doing more: looking for good variable names, explaining complex decision points, and writing code comments.

2.2.1 *Keep looking for good names*

Naming is a critical aspect of writing maintainable code. The more closely your code resembles how business people communicate, the better. Good variable names enable developers to quickly grasp a method's purpose and are particularly essential in information systems, as code should mirror business terminology.

Choosing an initial name for a variable, method, or class is tough. In a controlled experiment conducted by Feitelson, Mizrahi, and Noy (in "How Developers Choose Names," IEEE Transactions on Software Engineering, March 12, 2021), researchers noticed that if they ask two developers to name the same variable, they're likely to pick different names. That's why this pattern isn't about coming up with good variable names; it's about continually searching for the right name and refactoring until you find it.

When implementing a method, you may only have a vague idea of how a new variable will be used. Will it be combined with another variable, passed to another method, or returned to the caller? Because choosing initial names is difficult, I prefer not to dwell on them. I move forward, wait until I have more concrete code, and then focus on finding better variable and method names.

I often consider these questions when naming:

- Is the class name fitting and representative of the concept?
- Does the attribute name reveal its information while aligning with the class name?
- Does the method name clearly describe its function, expectations, and return?
- Is the interface name indicative of its concrete implementations' actions?
- Does the service name specify the actions it performs?

This list isn't exhaustive but aims to guide your naming considerations. You might initially answer yes to these questions, only to change your mind later. This is natural, especially during early development stages. So, don't hesitate to rename variables, methods, or classes repeatedly. Investing time in renaming saves future developers considerable effort.

> **Ubiquitous language**
>
> Popularized by domain-driven design, *ubiquitous language* refers to a shared and consistent language used by all development team members to communicate and understand domain concepts. This language should be reflected in the code. It helps eliminate confusion and ensure that everyone has a clear understanding of the problem domain. This is strongly related to what we just discussed.

2.2.2 Document decisions

A characteristic of information systems is that they make complex decisions based on lots of data. Because of that, decision points in the code can quickly become complex.

It's not uncommon to see `if` statements with multiple conditions. These `if` statements are crucial to the system; therefore, developers should be able to easily and quickly understand what they mean.

We can do several things to clarify decisions:

- Introduce extra variables in the code to better explain the meaning of complex `if` statements.
- Break the large and complex decision process into a set of smaller steps, each handling a smaller part of the process.
- Write a code comment that explains it.

Regardless of your approach, remember that clarifying the decisions a unit of code may make is vital for code legibility, as understanding the decision-making process eases maintenance and debugging.

2.2.3 Add code comments

Code comments written in natural language can be powerful, and there are many reasons to write a code comment. Some developers argue that if a code comment is needed, the code isn't clear enough. Others claim that comments become deprecated quickly, or they see pointless code comments everywhere. Although all these points are valid and we should always try first to improve the legibility of the code through refactoring, there are still cases where refactoring isn't enough.

The first reason we may want to add code comments is to explain things that go beyond the code. Clean code is excellent for explaining implementation details but isn't great for explaining the whys. For example, what was the business reason behind the decisions made in this code? Why did we take approach A instead of B?

Some may say that this information fits best on an internal wiki page. Wikis are great tools because we can write text with formatting. I prefer to write code comments as developers are always in their IDEs, closer to the code. I've seen teams add comments that link to a page in their internal wikis. This is also a good solution that combines the power of both tools.

Another reason we may prefer comments is that breaking the code into smaller pieces sometimes reduces rather than increases its readability. For example, an extract-method refactoring can sometimes make the code look cumbersome, especially if the code in the middle relies on numerous variables from preceding or subsequent sections. This can be evident when you use automated refactoring in your IDE, which may propose a private method with a strange signature or fail.

Separating blocks of code with code comments is a great way to explain the upcoming code. It's easy for a developer to identify different blocks of comments, so it's also easy for them to skip to the next block if they don't need to read that part of the code (see figure 2.2).

Finally, comments can save time for developers. In many cases, reading the name of the method and its parameters isn't enough to understand all of its details. Think of how often you've had a question about a method from a library. The name of the method was clear enough, but you still needed more information. Did you read its code, or did you read its documentation? I'd guess the documentation.

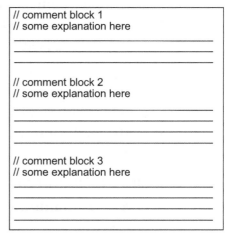

Figure 2.2   Comments separating code blocks

Open source methods are great examples of well-documented code. See, for example, the `WordUtils` class from the Apache Commons Lang (http://mng.bz/g7QR). All methods have long comments describing what they do.

Reading a summary of what the method does, its main caveats, what it does if preconditions aren't met, and so on is much faster than reading code. Remember that in most cases, you don't need to know the in-depth details of a method—only high-level information.

Although you may want to document every public method of an open source library that will be used by millions of developers, you shouldn't document every method in your software system: only those that contain complex business rules or have been through interesting decision-making processes. Understanding the "why" behind coding decisions is crucial for maintaining that piece of code in the future.

Now, let's talk about the problems with comments. A significant disadvantage is that they can become deprecated without anyone noticing. However, deprecated comments occur when those comments aren't essential. Developers usually (or at least should) update crucial comments. If you identify a comment that no one bothers to update, delete it.

Writing code with newcomers in mind is essential. A useless code comment may seem pointless to you, but it could help someone who's never seen the code before. Nevertheless, if you find a comment *truly* useless, delete it.

NOTE In *A Philosophy of Software Design,* by John Ousterhout (Yaknyam Press, 2018), he offers a refreshing perspective on code comments. His views on their importance and usefulness are worth exploring. I highly recommend reading his ideas on this topic.

2.2.4   *Example: Deciding when to send an update email*

Whenever an administrator updates an offering in PeopleGrow!, all employees who are enrolled for that offering should receive an email. At least, that's how the feature started. The business later noticed that employees were getting spammed by a large number of emails. If an administrator changes the number of available positions for a trainer, a participant doesn't need to know about it.

It was agreed that updates would be sent only if the offering's dates or description changed: imagine a text field where admins add the room where a training course will happen or a Zoom link. Employees can still opt in if they want to receive all updates.

Listing 2.4   Deciding whether an employee should receive an update email

```
public void update(UpdatedOffering updatedOffering) {

  // ...
  // logic to update the offering
  // ...

  if(employee.wantsAnyEmailUpdates() ||
     (updatedOffering.isDateUpdated() ||         ◁─── This if statement is too long
     updatedOffering.isDescriptioUpdated())) {        and needs more clarity.

    // send an update email to the employee

  }
}
```

The `if` statement is hard to understand. You have to dive into the code to follow what this decision point is all about.

Let's refactor this snippet as follows:

1. Separate the decision from the code that sends the email. Let's move the entire decision process to a `boolean shouldReceiveAnEmail()` method.

2. Introduce variables to explain the different parts of the `if` statement, simplifying its legibility.

3. Make the `Offering` class encapsulate the decision logic around whether important information was updated in an `isImportantInfoUpdated()` method. This way, if this logic ever changes, we only have to change it in a single place.

In the refactored version, it is much easier to understand what the method does. You can read the comments and understand how the implementation works because the complex `if` is broken down.

Listing 2.5   Better version of the algorithm

```
class Offering {
  // ...

  public boolean isImportantInfoUpdated() {
    return this.isDateUpdated() || this.isDescriptionUpdated();
  }
}


/**
 * An employee should receive an email in case
 * they opt-in for it or in case important information was updated.
 */
boolean shouldReceiveAnEmail(Offering updatedOffering,
  Employee employee) {

  boolean importantInfoWasUpdated = offering.isImportantInfoUpdated();
  boolean employeeWantsUpdates = employee.wantsAnyEmailUpdates();

  return employeeWantsUpdates || importantInfoWasUpdated;
}

...

if(shouldReceiveAnEmail(offering, employee)) {
  // send an update email to the student
}
```

Offering now offers a method that returns whether important information (right now, date or description) was updated.

The code comment explains what the method does.

The introduced variables help us break down the complex decision.

The complex decision is hidden in the shouldReceiveAnEmail method, so the developer doesn't have to read it unless they go to the implementation of the method.

Don't be afraid of documenting your code. Documentation is key to productive maintenance.

2.3   *Move new complexity away from existing classes*

> *Move any new complexity arising from feature requests or code evolution to a separate location. This pattern fosters simplicity and cohesiveness within existing units, making them easier to maintain and comprehend.*

Deciding when to create a new class while evolving code can be challenging. It's tempting to keep adding code where the rest of it already exists. However, continuously avoiding this question leads to lengthy and complex code.

Methods and classes that grow indefinitely eventually become unmaintainable. They should expand as business complexity increases, but this growth must be controlled. Overgrown code units eventually become too complex for developers to maintain with reasonable effort, resulting in complex classes.

In many cases, classes grow indefinitely due to a lack of good abstraction or extension points that enable developers to add new behavior without changing existing code. I'll cover these topics in chapters 4 and 5. In this section, I focus on two recurrent design decisions to avoid classes growing forever: move complex business rules to their own class, and break down large business flows into multiple steps.

2.3.1   *Give the complex business logic a class of its own*

Whenever there's a new complex business logic to implement, trying to fit it into an existing class can be a burden. We may never be able to find the suitable class because the rule spans multiple classes. We may also have to add too many other dependencies to an existing class because the rule will likely require interaction with many other classes.

In such cases, it's best to create another class that isolates the feature, keeping the other classes free from growing in complexity. There are a few advantages to doing that:

- Dedicating an entire class to a complex feature makes it easier to see all its dependencies. In this case, email-related classes and different repositories are explicitly listed in the service's constructor.
- The feature's code is isolated from the rest of the system. When reading the code, there's no need to separate what belongs to this feature and what doesn't, reducing cognitive overload.
- Isolation also makes testing easier. We can write tests for this feature without worrying about other behaviors.
- It simplifies reusing the functionality. This class can be called from any part of the system that needs the same functionality.
- The class is highly cohesive, doing only one thing.

A caveat is that at the same time, you should keep your business logic as close as possible to the class it acts on and not a class that's "far away," as I just said. For example, marking the `Enrollment` as canceled should happen inside the `Enrollment` class and not outside. We'll discuss encapsulation, state, and consistency in chapter 3.

2.3.2   *Break down large business flows*

Some long, complex methods exist because they control sizeable multiple-step business flows. Without a proper abstraction to help us model the flow, we may end up with a huge class where each method is one step of the flow. Imagine a business flow composed of 10, 15, or 20 steps. Putting the implementation of all steps in a single class isn't a good idea.

You should break down large, complex business flows into simple, small, cohesive units of code and use intelligent design mechanisms to deliver the entire flow. If each step is in its own class, you get all the benefits of small classes again:

- They are simple and easier to understand.
- They are easier to maintain.
- They are more easily testable.
- They can be better reused.

Although there are frameworks for organizing workflows, a simple abstraction often suffices. If you need patterns for breaking up multistep business flows, consider Gang of Four design patterns like Chain of Responsibility, Decorator, and Observer. You might also explore domain events for highly complex business flows (www.martinfowler .com/eaaDev/DomainEvent.html).

Another alternative is to build an event-based system, where each process step generates an event consumed by the next step. Consider this option for complex workflows requiring flexibility or when steps should occur in different services. Otherwise, stick to simpler workflow mechanisms. I won't delve into event-based system implementation details, as many books cover this topic (choose any microservices book).

Single Responsibility Principle

The Single Responsibility Principle (SRP) states that a class (or a method or any unit of code in general) should have one and only one reason to change. Cohesive classes and methods are much easier to understand and maintain.

The ideas discussed in this chapter are related to the SRP. After all, smaller units of code tend to be more cohesive than large units of code.

The key difference between the SRP and this chapter is that SRP focuses on dividing code according to their different responsibilities. Cohesive code should always be our north star. However, in many cases, it's hard to decide what the responsibilities of a class or method are, especially at the beginning of the development. Focusing on making units of code small is a more straightforward rule that you can apply from day one, even if you still don't know much about the software you're building. Once you identify that the class isn't cohesive enough, you should refactor it, and your job will be much easier because the classes and methods are small.

2.3.3 Example: Waiting list for offerings

PeopleGrow! offers a waiting list feature. If an offering is full, employees can join the waiting list. If someone unenrolls, the entire waiting list is notified, and the first employee who enrolls gets that spot. An employee who enrolls in an offering is automatically removed from the waiting list.

Let's focus on the part where someone unenrolls, and we need to send an email to all employees on the waiting list. The first implementation proposed by the developer was to implement this functionality in the UnenrollEmployeeFromOfferingService service. The service would retrieve the employees on the waiting list and then loop through this list and create an email for every one of them. Here's the initial implementation.

Listing 2.6 Notifying the waiting list when an employee unenrolls

```
class UnenrollEmployeeFromOfferingService {

  private Emailer emailer;
  private OfferingRepository offerings;

  public UnenrollEmployeeFromOfferingService(...,
    OfferingRepository offerings,
    Emailer emailer) {
    this.offerings = offerings;           One extra dependency
    this.emailer = emailer;           ◁—  to send the email
  }
```

```
public void unenroll(int enrollmentId) {
  // ...
  // logic to unenroll the employee
  // ...

  Offering offering = offerings.getOfferingFrom(enrollmentId);
  notifyWaitingList(offering);
}

private void notifyWaitingList(Offering offering) {
  Set<Employee> employees = offering.getWaitingList();
  for(Employee employee : employees) {
    emailer.sendWaitingListEmail(offering, employee);
  }
}
}
```

The new step on the flow, notify the waiting list, is now at the end of the unenroll process.

The notifyWaitingList private method implements the notification logic.

Adding this implementation to the existing `UnenrollEmployeeFrom-OfferingService` isn't a good idea, as it makes the class more complex. As soon we add `notifyWaitingList`, we may be forced to review all our automated tests for the `UnenrollEmployeeFromOfferingService` and see if they still work. Writing tests for the new feature in isolation is also more demanding.

A better option is to move the waiting list notification logic to a separate class, say, `WaitingListNotifier`. Move the complexity away from existing classes, as I said.

That's what we'll do. `UnenrollEmployeeFromOfferingService` now depends on the new `WaitingListNotifier` and calls when it's time to notify the employees. The waiting list notifier depends on `Emailer` and has the same logic as before.

Listing 2.7 Waiting list notification in another class

```
class UnenrollEmployeeFromOfferingService {

  private OfferingRepository offerings;
  private WaitingListNotifier notifier;

  public UnenrollEmployeeFromOfferingService(...,
    OfferingRepository offerings,
    WaitingListNotifier notifier) {
    this.offerings = offerings;
    this.notifier = notifier;
  }

  public void unenroll(int enrollmentId) {
```

The service depends on the new waiting list notifier.

```
  // ...
  // logic to unenroll the employee
  // ...

  Offering offering = offerings.getOfferingFrom(enrollmentId);
  notifier.notify(offering);          ◁────┐  Calls the new notifier class
  }
}

class WaitingListNotifier {

  private Emailer emailer;
                                              The new class depends
  public WaitingListNotifier(Emailer emailer) {  ◁──┘ on the Emailer.
    this.emailer = emailer;
  }
                                              The notification logic
  public void notify(Offering offering) {   ◁──┘ is in the new class.
    Set<Employee> employees = offering.getWaitingList();
    for(Employee employee : employees) {
      emailer.sendWaitingListEmail(offering, employee);
    }
  }
}
```

Figure 2.3 illustrates the new class design. Note how we managed to move new complexity away from existing classes. We did so by creating a new class and delegating this new behavior to it. The new class is also small, easily testable, and reusable. This simple pattern works more often than you'd expect. We achieved a simpler design by forcing ourselves to move new complexity away from existing code.

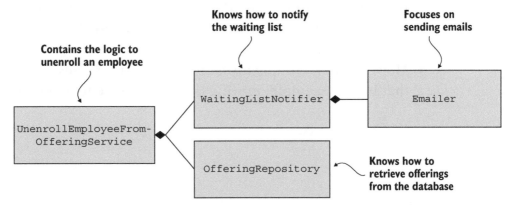

Figure 2.3 A set of smaller classes work together to deliver the unenrolling-employee feature,

2.4   *Exercises*

Think through the following questions or discuss them with a colleague:

1 If you were to define a hard threshold for the maximum number of lines of code that a method can have, what would it be? Why?

2 How do you currently document your software systems? Does your approach work? Do you see room for improvement?

3 Have you ever encountered bad comments in code? What about good code comments? What did both look like?

4 This chapter strongly argues for small classes. What are your thoughts? Do you also prefer having many small classes instead of a larger class, or do you see advantages in larger classes?

Summary

- Code complexity arises when code units become too large and complex to understand, maintain, and extend, leading to bugs.

- To reduce code complexity, break down complex methods and classes into smaller ones, such as splitting a large method into smaller private methods or moving code to different classes.

- Use explanatory variables, clear method names, and natural language comments to make code easy for other developers to read. Code comments should explain why decisions were made, and easy-to-read code should explain the implementation logic.

- Move any new complexity away from existing units. You can do that by, for example, moving the new feature to a new class.

Keeping objects consistent

3

This chapter covers

- Keeping classes consistent
- Modeling aggregates that hold complex object relationships
- Implementing validation mechanisms that ensure consistency at all times

A well-designed class encapsulates its data and provides operations to access or manipulate it. These operations ensure that the object remains in a valid state without inconsistencies. Better yet, they do so in a way that the clients of the class don't even need to know about it.

One of the greatest advantages of object-oriented programming is the ability to ensure that objects are always in a consistent state. Compare it with, say, procedural programming languages like C. In C, you can define data structures (known as *structs*). However, there's no way to control who changes the values inside the structs. Any piece of code, anywhere in the codebase, can change them.

When code is not appropriately encapsulated, developers feel they can never find where to patch the code or fully fix a bug in one shot. When code is spread out and not encapsulated, developers have to constantly search for things. Just going to the class that defines the abstraction isn't enough. A developer may find a place to fix the code, only to have the same bug appear somewhere else.

Encapsulation, the idea of keeping data within the object and allowing users to manipulate it only through elegant operations, is the cornerstone of object-oriented programming. It's due to encapsulation that we can change internal details of a class without affecting the rest of the codebase. In this chapter, I present some patterns that will help you design classes that will stay consistent no matter what.

Consistency or integrity?

In object-oriented programming, the word *consistency* is commonly used to indicate that an object has accurate and reliable information. In other computer science domains, such as databases, the term *integrity* refers to the accuracy of the information (and *consistency* is often related to the availability of the data).

3.1   *Ensure consistency at all times*

> *Ensure that objects are in a consistent state at all times. This improves reliability, because objects are always in a valid state regardless of where and how they are being used.*

When objects are consistent, their internal state is synchronized and coherent with the program's requirements and users' expectations. Maintaining consistency ensures that objects behave correctly and produce accurate results, leading to reliable and trustworthy software.

The rule of thumb when it comes to consistency is this: Does the client of the class need to work to be sure the object is in a consistent state? If yes, you likely have a poorly designed class that may soon haunt you. Maintaining a consistent state should take minimal, if not zero, effort from clients. In the following sections, we explore patterns that make encapsulation a breeze.

3.1.1 *Make the class responsible for its consistency*

You should ensure that consistency checks are coded in the class itself. If you're not sure which class should maintain data consistency, a good rule of thumb is to always make the class that contains the data also ensure its consistency.

In information systems, entities are usually the classes containing the data. For example, making sure an `Offering` never accepts more participants than its maximum allowed limit should happen inside the `Offering` class, as should reducing the number of empty seats by one as soon as someone enrolls. The developers who use these classes shouldn't have to say "I just added one more participant to the offering. Now I need to reduce the number of available spots by one."

Figure 3.1 illustrates the idea. Stay alert. If you find yourself coding consistency checks outside the class, pause and reconsider.

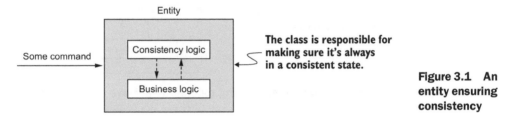

Figure 3.1   An entity ensuring consistency

Can consistency always be ensured inside the class? Unfortunately, no.

3.1.2 *Encapsulate entire actions and complex consistency checks*

Some consistency checks need information beyond that in the object, or they may be too complex, requiring the code to live somewhere outside the class. For example, we may need to consult the information in the database to decide whether an operation is valid. We can't do (and shouldn't want to do) that from inside the entity.

NOTE Technically, you can access the database from an entity, and some frameworks—especially those that support Active Record, like Ruby on Rails—make it easy to do so. However, this is not the standard in most architectures and is something we usually avoid.

In these cases, we should encapsulate the consistency checks and the business logic in one class: for example, in service classes, as described in chapter 1. Services ensure the consistency that entities can't provide themselves, although entities still ensure as much as they can on their own. Figure 3.2 illustrates the overall idea of this pattern.

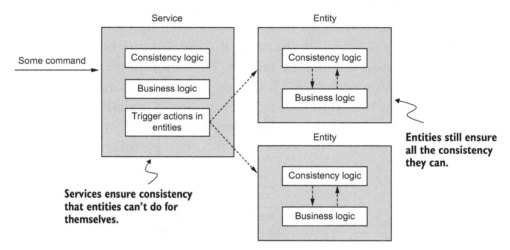

Figure 3.2   Services and entities working together to achieve consistency

The advantage of moving all the consistency logic to a new class is that we can implement complex consistency checks without making the original (entity) class more complex. The clear disadvantage is that when we move this logic away from the class it's supposed to be in, clients of the class need to know that they should use the service.

Documentation plays an important role here. You should write code comments in the most natural places a developer will look if they want that behavior. For example, the Offering entity may deserve a comment saying that if a client wants to add an employee to a training course, it should use the service class.

Although it's sad to see behavior separated from data, sometimes it's necessary. Clients should never be responsible for consistency checks; the class should manage it by default. If checks are too complex for the class, move the entire operation, including consistency checks, to a service class, and require clients to use this class for the desired behavior.

NOTE Later in this chapter, I talk more about aggregate roots, as moving behavior to another class becomes tricky if the class is an aggregate of multiple classes and has many invariants to take care of.

The complexity of the consistency checks is an excellent reason to move the process to another class. There may be other good reasons. Avoiding unwanted dependencies is one of them. I'll talk more about class dependencies in future chapters, but I like my domain classes to be as pure as possible and contain only data and methods that operate on this data. I especially avoid coupling domain classes to classes that access things like databases or other external software systems. As a rule of thumb, the object should take care of all the consistency checks it can without relying on additional dependencies.

3.1.3 *Example: The Employee entity*

An offering in PeopleGrow! contains the date it will happen, the list of employees attending the training course, the maximum number of participants allowed, and an open description text field where administrators can write information like the room where the training course will happen, a Zoom link, and so on.

The first version of the `Offering` class is shown in listing 3.1. Note that the class doesn't ensure consistency. This is a poorly designed class, as it's easy to put it in an inconsistent state. Clients have to check whether there are available spots before adding an employee and then, later, reduce the number of available spots by one (see listing 3.2). Imagine a client forgetting to update the number of available spots. Suddenly the object is invalid.

Also note `setAvailableSpots`, which sets a new number without checking whether it's valid. This is not good.

Listing 3.1 The `Offering` entity

```
class Offering {
    private int id;                          The id field contains the
    private Training training;               database ID of this offering.
    private Calendar date;
    private Set<Employee> employees;
    private int maximumNumberOfAttendees;
    private int availableSpots;
```

```
public Offering(
  Training training,
  Calendar date,
  int maximumNumberOfAttendees,
  int availableSpots) {
  this.training = training;
  this.date = date;
  this.maximumNumberOfAttendees = maximumNumberOfAttendees;
  this.availableSpots = maximumNumberOfAttendees;
}

public Set<Employee> getEmployees() {
  return this.employees;
}

public int getAvailableSpots() {
  return this.availableSpots;
}

public void setAvailableSpots(int availableSpots) {
  this.availableSpots = availableSpots;
}
}
```

The constructor stores the information passed in the attributes of the class.

The number of available spots is the same as the maximum number of attendees when the object is created.

Returns the list of employees in the offering

A getter ...

... and a setter for the number of available spots

Listing 3.2 Clients using the `Offering` entity

```
Offering offering = getOfferingFromDatabase();

if(offering.getNumberOfAvailableSpots() > 0) {
  offering.getEmployees().add(employeeThatWantsToParticipate);
  offering.setAvailableSpots(offering.getAvailableSpots() - 1);
}
```

Suppose an offering comes from the database.

Are spots available in the training course?

Adds the employee to the offering

Reduces the number of available spots by 1

The first refactoring we must do makes the `Offering` class ensure its internal consistency. This means the class should make sure the number of available spots is reduced by one if someone is added to the training course. The class also should not allow a new employee to join the training course if it's already full.

The new version of the class in listing 3.3 has a much better `addEmployee` method. The method ensures that no one can be added to the training course if it doesn't have any empty spots. The method also keeps tabs on the number of available spots. Now the clients of this class don't need to know anything about how offerings work. Whenever they want to add an employee, they call `addEmployee()` and move forward.

Listing 3.3 `Offering` **entity with the new** `addEmployee()` **method**

```
class Offering {

  private int id;
  private Training training;
  private Calendar date;
  private Set<Employee> employees;
  private int maximumNumberOfAttendees;
  private int availableSpots;

  public Offering(Training training, Calendar date,
    int maximumNumberOfAttendees) {
    // basic constructor
  }

  public void addEmployee(Employee employee) {     ◁──┐ Ensures that the object
    if(availableSpots == 0)                             is always consistent
      throw new OfferingIsFullException();

    employees.add(employee);
    availableSpots--;
  }
                                          ┌── It's still fine to let clients know
  public int getAvailableSpots() {    ◁──┘   how many spots are available.
    return this.availableSpots;
  }
}
```

It's also important to notice that the class doesn't offer the `getEmploy-ees` method. We don't want clients to be able to handle an internal data structure of the class by themselves without any control. Only `Offering` should handle the list of employees.

Returning a copy of the data structure

One way to avoid giving clients full access to an internal data structure of the object—as in this case, where we don't want to give access to the internal list of employees—is to instead give them a copy of that data structure. Changes they make in the copy won't affect the original data structure, which is only available internally to the object. I discuss when and how to offer getters and setters later in this chapter.

We can also improve the construction of the class. The class shouldn't allow an `Offering` to be created with an empty training course or a negative number of `maximumNumberOfAttendees`. I talk more about this when we discuss validation in the next section.

> ## Concurrency and design
>
> Don't forget that nonfunctional requirements may influence your design decisions. For example, if you expect multiple simultaneous requests to add employees to training courses, listing 3.3 may not work, as there will be concurrent access to `availableSpots`. To solve this problem in an information system where multiple requests may be processed at the same time, you can ensure that requests for the same training course are processed linearly through, say, smart queueing. Or, in terms of class design, you can get rid of `availableSpots` and eliminate concurrent access to this field.
>
> I won't dive into architectural patterns for data-intensive systems in this book. But the overall message is that you should never forget your functional and nonfunctional requirements when designing classes.

3.2 *Design effective data validation mechanisms*

Validate client data to prevent unexpected errors and reduce the risk of odd behavior in the system. Clearly define the consequences of invalid data. This pattern improves code reliability and user experience by ensuring that the system can better handle and communicate problems.

Validating data throughout your system may seem tedious, but it pays off in the long run. Consider what will happen if a user requests the creation of a training course offering with an empty date. Will the software crash, or will it handle the invalid input gracefully?

I discuss two design approaches to handle data validation in the following sections. One focuses on explicitly defining pre- and post-conditions of methods, and the other validates input data from a business perspective.

3.2.1 *Make preconditions explicit*

Many bugs and inconsistencies in software systems occur when methods call other methods in invalid ways. This can happen for various reasons, such as not knowing how to use a class or method, or input data cascading from previous code layers without prechecks.

The second reason is harder to spot in code. Systems have complex data flows, and we can't be aware of all of them. By actively ensuring pre- and postconditions and explicitly documenting them, we reduce the chances of inconsistent program execution and increase the likelihood of others using classes as intended.

Let's start with preconditions. Methods should make it clear what values are valid for each input. For example, the Offering class offers a method called addEmployee that receives Employees as a parameter. The method adds the employee to that course.

What if the client passes null to the method? Null is clearly an invalid input parameter. If nothing is done, the system will likely crash at some point. It's the developer's responsibility to decide what the method should do if a client doesn't respect the preconditions of a method.

We can design different actions when preconditions aren't met. We can take harsh measures against invalid input values, such as throwing an exception. Throwing an exception has an advantage: it halts the program right away. Halting the program is better than continuing its execution when we don't know how to proceed with the invalid data. However, this decision increases the workload for client classes because they have to handle this possible exception. If that's our intention for that class, it's a perfect decision.

In other cases, we may choose a more lightweight way of handling preconditions. For example, the method can accept nulls and do nothing in these cases. If a null comes in, the method returns early. This option requires less effort from clients because the method doesn't throw exceptions or stop working in case of invalid input (which is no longer invalid because the method can handle it).

Handling invalid input was easy in this example, but it may require more lines of code in practice. The tradeoff is that if we make our code more tolerant toward bad input, saving clients from handling possible exceptions themselves, the method's developer must code a bit more.

Overall, explicitly thinking of preconditions is a fundamental design activity that will save our code from crashing unexpectedly. This is one of the few practices discussed in this book that focuses more on quality as in, "This code works"—rather than quality as in, "This code is easy to maintain." However, code that works is easier to maintain.

Additionally, the maintenance aspect is related to how we decide to handle the precondition. In his book *A Philosophy of Software Design*, John Ousterhout says we should "define errors out of existence." For example, imagine a method that returns all employees enrolled in a training course. Instead of throwing an exception if no employees are enrolled, we can return an empty list. Or imagine a method that marks an invoice as paid. If the invoice is already paid, instead of throwing an exception if someone tries to mark it as paid again, the code does nothing. By simplifying the preconditions of the code, we simplify the lives of our clients because they have fewer corner cases to handle.

If you can design your code so that it can't fail, that's better for maintenance. If you consider that you'll develop the class once, but it will be used multiple times by different clients, saving them effort is also a good thing to do in the long run.

3.2.2 *Create validation components*

In enterprise systems, actions often require more than just meeting method preconditions. Take enrolling in a training course as an example. addEmployee has a simple precondition: don't accept nulls. However, from a business perspective, there might be additional validations: employees can't take the same course more than three times, the employee must be from a specific office, and so on. These rules aren't preconditions per se, but we must ensure that the request complies with them.

Business validation rules are pervasive in enterprise systems, so you should handle validation explicitly in your code by giving rules their own classes. This enables reusability and clarity when clients call validation methods.

> **Preconditions vs. validation rules**
> Preconditions are the minimum requirements for a unit of code to execute correctly, such as "This attribute can't be null" or "This value should be A, B, or C." Validation rules are more business related and often require more code for checks, like "Employees can't take the same training course more than three times."

We don't want clients to handle consistency or precondition checks, and we don't want them to know that validation rules should be called before an action. In this case, it's also wise to design a service class to control the flow and ensure that validations and consistency checks happen before the action.

Figure 3.3 enhances the previous figure. Services do consistency and validation checks that entities can't. Services may get the help of validation components. Entities still perform all the consistency checks they can.

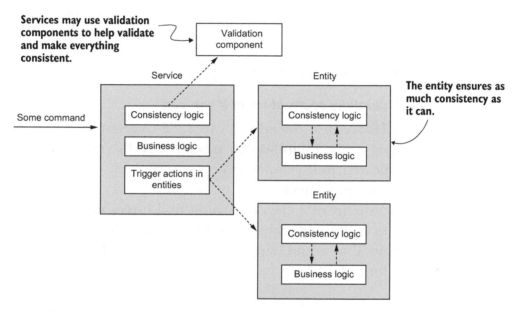

Figure 3.3   Validation components help maintain consistency.

Let me make a few final remarks about validation classes:

- If you're sure you'll need to reuse the same validation rules for other use cases or service classes, design them so they can be reusable elsewhere. If you are looking for a way to build flexible validation rules, consider the Specification pattern, which became popular after the book *Domain-Driven Design* by Eric Evans was published in 2003. This pattern allows you to define rules and compose them in different ways. However, most validation rules are specific to a feature or service. Don't overdesign validation classes.

- Should you call validation components from inside an entity? Because many validation rules require external dependencies such as databases, and you don't want to couple your entities to such things, it's preferable not to call them from an entity. Using a service class to coordinate is a worthwhile tradeoff for complex business actions.
- If you try to instantiate an entity that does all the proper consistency checks directly with the data from the user, you may get an immediate precondition violation without having the chance to do other checks. To avoid this, you can introduce intermediate classes like `OfferingForm`, which are data structures that hold the user's data without validation. Once the data is valid, you can convert it to a proper `Offering` class.

3.2.3 *Use nulls carefully or avoid them if you can*

Sir Tony Hoare introduced nulls in 1965 as a convenient solution, later calling it his "billion-dollar mistake." Nulls can be tricky, causing unexpected null pointer exceptions and hindering readability with excessive null checks.

The possibility of a class returning null forces clients to perform null checks everywhere, which hampers readability. In the following listing, note what would happen if we had to check for nulls at every point in the code.

Listing 3.4 Null checks everywhere

```
var obj1 = method1();           ◁———  method1() may return a null,
if(obj1!=null) {                       forcing the code to do a check.
  var obj2 = method2();

  if(obj2!=null) {
    var obj3 = method3();

    if(obj3!=null) {            ◁———  Look how deep this code already
      // ... code continues ...        is, just because of three checks.
    }
  }
}
```

This example may be extreme, but I hope you get the point. Adding null checks everywhere is something you should avoid.

The best thing you can do is ensure that your methods never return null. How? Consider the following:

- If a method has a path that should return nothing, consider creating an object that represents nothing. For example, if the method returns a list, will it be a problem if you return an empty list if the operation isn't successful?
- If you want to return null because there was a problem in the execution of a method, should this method then throw an exception? Can you make the method return a class that describes the problem?
- Can you design the error out of existence? For example, if the client passes a null to a list parameter, can you assume this list is empty instead of returning null?
- If a method returns null because a library you don't control returns nulls, can you wrap this library call and transform the result?

A system without null returns is easier to work with, but avoiding nulls requires time and effort. We have to invest some time in designing away the null.

What if you need to represent the absence of information? Isn't that what null is all about? Languages like Java offer the `Optional` type, which can be helpful in such situations. Clients must check for the presence of a value before proceeding.

I also don't want to discard the need for a null return you can't control. Life is hard, and you may be in one of those situations. If so, I suggest documenting the behavior so clients know they must be prepared for it. Avoiding surprises is the best you can do when you can't model away a null.

Tools can also help you identify pieces of code that may suffer from null pointers. For example, the Checker Framework and IntelliJ's null-detection capabilities are excellent at detecting places where you should handle a possible null return.

3.2.4   *Example: Adding an employee to a training offering*

PeopleGrow! has many business rules around adding an employee to an offering:

- An employee can't register if there are no spots available.
- An employee can't take the same course more than three times.
- An employee can't be registered more than once for the same offering.

These rules can't all be implemented inside the `Offering` class, as a single instance of an offering doesn't have access to whether the employee already took this course in the past. Given that adding an employee to an offering has become more complex, the entity isn't the best place to code this rule. We need a service and a validation class.

Let's start with the service class. Its implementation should be straightforward. We validate the request. If it's valid, we add the employee to the offering.

As a design choice, I opted to receive the IDs of the offering and the employee and let the service retrieve them from the database. Another option would be to receive the `Offering` and `Employee` entities directly, forcing the client to retrieve them before calling the service. Both approaches have advantages and disadvantages.

The method then ensures that both exist in the database; otherwise, it throws an error. Then it calls the `AddEmployeeToOfferingValidator` validator to ensure that this is a valid request from a business point of view. (Can we implement the validation rules in the service directly? If they are simple, sure. If they are more complex, I prefer a dedicated class, as discussed earlier.) If validation goes fine, we add the employee to the offering. If not, we throw an exception.

> **Listing 3.5** `AddEmployeeToOfferingService` **class**

```
class AddEmployeeToOfferingService {

  private OfferingRepository offerings;
  private EmployeeRepository employees;
  private AddEmployeeToOfferingValidator validator;

  public void addEmployee(int offeringId, int employeeId) {

    var offering = offerings.findById(offeringId);
```

```
    var employee = employees.findById(employeeId);

    if(offering == null || employe == null)
      throw new InvalidRequestException(
        "Offering and employee IDs should be valid");

    var validation = validator.validate(offering, employee);
    if(validation.hasErrors()) {
      throw new ValidationException(validation);
    }

    offering.addEmployee(employee);
  }
}
```

Checks whether the offering and employee IDs are valid

Calls out the validator to ensure that this is a valid request business-wise

If validation fails, throws an exception and lets the client handle it

Adds the employee to the offering

Depending on your architecture and technologies of choice, the service may also have to handle other aspects of your system. For example, suppose you choose an object-relational mapper (ORM) such as Hibernate. In that case, you don't have to call an update method explicitly to persist the changes in the database, as Hibernate will handle that for you. If you aren't using an ORM, you may have to explicitly call methods that will persist the change in the database.

Naming services

Naming is a tough software engineering problem. I decided to name this service after the action it provides ("add an employee to an offering") because it makes the intent and functionality of the service immediately evident to developers and domain experts. People name services in different ways. Pick whichever makes the intent of that service the most evident.

This snippet doesn't explicitly show how the service should be instantiated. Depending on how you design everything, you may use a dependency injection framework or do it manually.

The implementation of the `AddEmployeeToOfferingValidator` class is also straightforward. It contains a sequence of `if`s, each checking a business rule, and notes if the request is invalid.

Listing 3.6 `AddEmployeeToOfferingValidator` class

```
class AddEmployeeToOfferingValidator {

  private TrainingRepository trainings;
```

```
public ValidationResult validate(
  Offering offering,
  Employee employee) {

  var validation = new ValidationResult();

  if(!offering.hasAvailableSpots()) {
    validation.addError("Offering has no available spots.");
  }

  var timesParticipantTookTheTraining =
    trainings.countParticipations(employee, offering.getTraining())

  if(timesParticipantTookTheTraining >= 3) {
    validation.addError("Participant can't take the training again.");
  }

  if(offering.isEmployeeRegistered(employee)) {
    validation.addError("Participant already in this offering.");
  }

  return validation;
  }
}
```

The offering must have available spots.

The participant shouldn't have taken the course more than 3 times.

The participant can't be already in this offering.

I won't go into the details of ValidationResult. Just imagine a simple class that stores the list of possible errors that the validator identifies. The service can then ask if there were errors (via validation.hasErrors()) and decide what to do with them: for example, repassing them to the client that called the service.

What matters in this listing is that the service coordinates the action and doesn't allow an invalid request to proceed. It makes sure offerings are always consistent.

This means clients shouldn't be able to call addEmployee() directly; only the service should be able to do that. In many programming languages, you can play with visibility modifiers, module systems, or even static analysis to prevent that from happening.

Note that you can implement the generic validation mechanism many different ways. Don't get too attached to my ValidationResult example. As I said before, make it simple, and evolve it over time.

> **Domain services and application services**
>
> Domain-driven design (DDD) and clean architecture distinguish between domain services and application services. Application services should only coordinate the work and have no business rules, whereas domain services contain the business rules. The latest version of `AddEmployeeToOfferingService` acts as an application service as it only coordinates the tasks between the different classes that are part of the operation and has no business rules.
>
> Separating application and domain services, or separating control flow from business logic, helps simplify your code and domain. As always, I take a pragmatic approach. I start with a simple service, and I'm lenient at the beginning if the service is playing the roles of both an application and a domain service. However, as soon as the complexity starts to grow, I refactor.

3.3 *Encapsulate state checks*

> *Encapsulate state checks, regardless of their complexity. Doing so ensures that clients remain ignorant about other classes' internal details, enabling classes to change their internal implementation without breaking the clients.*

Clients often need to know the object's state to make decisions. We're used to encapsulating business rules, but we often forget to also encapsulate state checks.

Consider asking if the `Offering` class still has spots available. An inattentive developer may write something like `if(offering.getNumberOfAvailableSpots() == 0)` (if the number of available spots is equal to zero) or even `offering.getEmployees().size() < offering.getNumberOfAvailableSpots()` (if the number of employees enrolled is smaller than the number of total spots).

Although this may work for a while, it creates a strong coupling between the `Offering` class and all the clients. What if the class internally changes the way it represents the number of available spots? Clients would have to be changed as well.

This design problem even has a name: *shotgun surgery* (https:// refactoring.guru/smells/shotgun-surgery). Shotgun surgeries happen whenever a change in one place requires several other places to change. Figure 3.4 illustrates. You should avoid shotgun surgeries as much as possible.

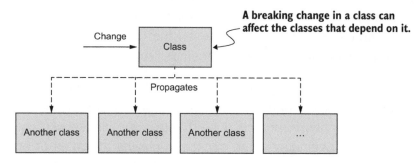

Figure 3.4   Shotgun surgery

Encapsulate the state check so the clients don't have to do any work. Make the `Offering` class offer a method like `boolean hasAvailableSpots()`. How the class implements it internally is no longer important for the clients. You can change the class's internal implementation as many times as you like.

Encapsulating state checks is crucial when they become more complex. You certainly don't want your clients to write complex `if` statements to get the information they need about the object's state.

Although writing state checks in client code may seem convenient, encapsulating even simple checks can save time and provide flexibility. This approach prevents clients from needing to understand the inner workings of the class, allowing the class to change freely.

3.3.1   *Tell, don't ask*

"Tell, don't ask" is a principle in object-oriented programming that encourages telling objects what to do instead of asking them for data and acting on it. You can read more about it on Martin Fowler's wiki (https://martinfowler.com/bliki/TellDontAsk.html).

We've seen that encapsulating state checks within objects is beneficial. However, if clients have to ask the object for information so they know how to act on it, there's room for improvement. For example, in the first version of the Offering class implemented in this chapter, we had to see if there were available spots (ask) and, if so, add the employee (tell). In the second version, clients had to tell the class to add the employee.

The latter approach is better for maintenance and evolution, as clients don't need to check whether the offering has spots before calling addEmployee. Moreover, if addEmployee requires additional checks in the future, we only need to modify it internally in the method and not in all the clients, avoiding shotgun surgery. This shouldn't surprise you, as we discussed similar things previously in this chapter, but now you know the name of a related principle.

3.3.2   *Example: Available spots in an offering*

If a client of our Offering class needs to know whether spots are still available, the client has to get the number of available spots via get-NumberOfAvailableSpots() and see if the number is greater than zero.

Let's better encapsulate this state check. The Offering class now has a hasAvailableSpots() method, which abstracts how the check is done away from clients. This allows the Offering class to change its implementation freely if needed.

The implementation of the method is as simple as availableSpots > 0. It doesn't matter that it's so simple: you should encapsulate it and free your clients from knowing how to do it.

> **Listing 3.7   Implementing the hasAvailableSpots method**

```
class Offering {

  // ...
  private int availableSpots;

  public boolean hasAvailableSpots() {      Checks if the number of available
    return availableSpots > 0;              spots is greater than 0
  }

  public int getAvailableSpots() {          It's still acceptable to have this
    return this.availableSpots;             getter, as some clients may need to
  }                                         know the number of spots available.
}
```

The Offering class is getting much better!

3.4   *Provide only getters and setters that matter*

> *Offer clients only relevant getters and setters. Getters should not modify or allow modification of the class state, and setters should be provided for descriptive properties only. This pattern promotes code clarity and maintainability by limiting the public interface of a class to what is necessary and relevant for clients.*

Getters and setters enable clients to access and modify class data. These methods are essential in languages like Java but less so in Python or C#, which offer different functionalities. Regardless of your programming language, you must prevent clients from having unrestricted access to attributes.

If classes can freely modify attributes, how can we ensure consistency? Additionally, if classes can access any attribute, how can we guarantee that future class evolutions won't break clients because they are now coupled to every attribute?

But we can't write software without offering clients ways to interact with class data. In the following two sections, we discuss the characteristics of good getters and setters.

3.4.1   *Getters that don't change state and don't reveal too much to clients*

Getters should never change the state of the class. This is an essential and unbreakable rule. Command-query separation (CQS) is a principle that says a method should be either a command (perform an action that changes the state of the system) or a query (return data to the caller) but never both.

Although this rule is generally well followed, it's crucial to think about which attributes should have getters. Some fields may be better kept inside the class or replaced with more elegant getters providing richer information.

The practical challenge with getters is that frameworks often require getters and setters for their functionality. Some developers separate classes for mapping objects to relational tables from domain classes to avoid breaking invariants. Others prefer a more pragmatic approach, providing the getter or setter the framework requires and understanding that the design doesn't fully protect against bad changes. It depends on developers using classes correctly. This has been less of a problem with modern frameworks that understand good object-oriented practices, but still, it is worth knowing, given that most of us still have legacy systems to maintain.

> ### Unmodifiable collections
> In Java, you can ensure that the returned list of employees is unmodifiable. If you have to offer a getter that returns a list, return an immutable collection.

3.4.2 Setters only to attributes that describe the object

Careless setters can lead to inconsistent objects, as they allow anyone to update the field of a class any way they want. Each setter in the code should exist only after a deliberate decision.

Never offer a setter for an attribute requiring consistency checks. Instead, provide elegant methods that safely perform the operation, like the `addEmployee()` method discussed earlier. We don't want clients to do `offering.getEmployees().add(employee)`.

A safe rule of thumb for using setters is when the attribute being changed mainly describes the object, such as a `description` attribute for an `Offering` class or a `name` attribute in an `Employee` class. Setters for descriptive fields usually won't cause future problems. For other fields, consider whether allowing changes could lead to inconsistency.

> ### Checks inside setters
> Setters can include additional code, like checking for null values before storing them. However, if you need business checks inside setters, consider giving the method a more meaningful name (or moving the operation to a service if the consistency check is complex). This way, your code follows the convention that setters only assign values, making it clear what to expect from any setter in your codebase.

3.4.3 Example: Getters and setters in the Offering class

The `Offering` class should offer clients the possibility of seeing the list of employees on an offering. However, we don't want clients to be able to change that list without going through the proper service.

There are many ways we could implement this. For example, we could create a method that returns a different data structure with the list of employees: say, an `EnrolledEmployees` class. This way, even if clients changed the data, it wouldn't be reflected in the entity.

I often use this approach, as it strongly decouples the entities from my model that I need to keep consistent from objects that only carry data. This approach also allows me to return only what the clients need. For example, maybe clients only need an employee's name and e-mail. The new data structure can only contain what clients need, decoupling them even more from the entity.

Your programming language may also offer a way to return copies of lists or even immutable data structures that throw exceptions if clients try to modify them. In this example, I use Java's way of returning an immutable collection. The `unmodifiableSet` method from the `Collections` class, part of Java's collections library, returns a list that can't be modified.

Listing 3.8 `getEmployees` returns an immutable list

```
class Offering {

  ...
  private Set<Employee> employees;

  public Set<Employee> getEmployees() {          ⟵——— This set is unmodifiable!
    return Collections.unmodifiableSet(employees);
  }
}
```

The `getEmployees` method is now a safe getter! Also note that we don't offer a `setEmployees` method, as allowing a client to pass an entire list of employees at once makes no sense.

Should we offer a setter for `maximumNumberOfAttendees`? I don't think so. Modifying the maximum number of attendees may involve logic. What if we have more employees in the offering than the new number? A simple setter isn't enough; we'd need a proper method in the `Offering` class or a service if the logic became more complex.

3.5   *Model aggregates to ensure invariants in clusters of objects*

> *Design aggregates to ensure consistency of entities that hold clusters of objects. This approach improves code clarity and maintainability, making it easier to reason about entities that handle complex relationships between objects.*

In DDD, an *aggregate root* is a cluster of objects treated as a single object by the rest of the application. The main object, or root, ensures consistency in the entire object tree. Clients can access and call operations only on the root object and not directly on its internal objects. Clients should hold references only to the aggregate, to prevent changes to internal objects without the root's knowledge. For example, a `Basket` class may be composed of multiple `Items` composed of `Products`, but the other classes of the system only see `Basket`. If they need the `Products` inside it, they will ask the aggregate root: in this case, the `Basket` class. Figure 3.5 illustrates.

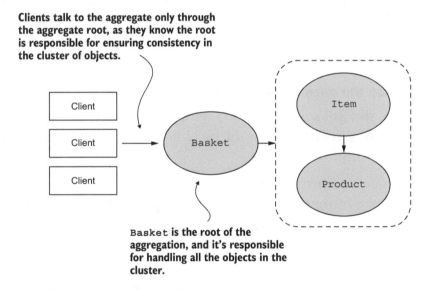

Clients talk to the aggregate only through the aggregate root, as they know the root is responsible for ensuring consistency in the cluster of objects.

`Basket` **is the root of the aggregation, and it's responsible for handling all the objects in the cluster.**

Figure 3.5   An aggregate root

As DDD suggests, modeling aggregate roots should be an explicit part of your design process. Identifying objects within an aggregate root and ensuring that they're accessed only through it is a crucial design activity that pays off in software maintenance. If all actions go through the aggregate root, it can maintain consistency throughout the object tree.

Note that aggregate roots go beyond simply encapsulating lists of objects. They do more than that. We're modeling entities that should be responsible for keeping the consistency of more complex domain relationships.

Another important rule with aggregates is treating aggregate roots as the unit to be passed around. When persisting an object to the database, pass the entire aggregate root, not a specific internal object. You should, therefore, have one repository or data access object per aggregate root, not per database entity. This maintains consistency by passing aggregate root references.

Regarding persistence, the aggregate root repository also ensures database integrity. For example, deleting an enrollment from an offering directly in the database using `enrollmentRepository.delete (enrollment)` might break consistency in the offering, as the number-of-available-spots field might now be incorrect. A well-designed `OfferingRepository` wouldn't offer a `deleteEnrollment` method because it could break consistency.

3.5.1   *Don't break the rules of an aggregate root*

Trust me: you will sometimes feel tempted to skip the aggregate root and operate directly on one of its child objects. There are various reasons for this:

- Some frameworks or libraries may require it, such as persistence frameworks needing one repository per database entity.
- For performance reasons, you might prefer to access a small part of the aggregate directly rather than through the aggregate root.
- Aggregate roots with deep object clusters may need too much boilerplate code for simple changes.

Are you willing to sacrifice consistency and maintainability for other benefits? My advice is to be pragmatic. Use all available tools and software to your advantage, but be aware of the tradeoffs.

The personal checklist I go through whenever I feel tempted to break an aggregate root is as follows:

- Is the benefit from breaking the aggregate rules much more beneficial than keeping maintenance costs low and invariants always up to date?
- If I want to change part of the aggregate directly without going through the aggregate root, am I sure this object should be part of the aggregate? If no real invariant needs to be kept, break the aggregate into smaller parts.
- If there's an invariant to be kept, can I still break the aggregate root and accept that there will be some eventual consistency between the two aggregates? You can use domain events to ensure the aggregate is notified about the change in the other aggregate.

NOTE This discussion only scratches the surface of designing aggregate roots. Consider reading books on DDD, such as Eric Evans' *Domain-Driven Design* and Vaughn Vernon's *Implementing Domain-Driven Design* (Addison-Wesley Professional, 2013) for deeper exploration.

3.5.2 *Example: The Offering aggregate*

PeopleGrow! needs to improve how offerings are handled. Right now, we store the list of employees in a training course, and if an employee drops out, we remove them from the list. The business wants to know the date the employee enrolled for that course, as well as the date of the unenrollment if the employee drops out of the course.

Storing employees as a simple list isn't enough. We need another entity to store the extra required information. Let's call this entity `Enrollment`. An enrollment will contain the employee, the date of enrollment, the enrollment status, and, if canceled, the date of cancellation.

The `Enrollment` class stores all the information for an enrollment. It also offers a `cancel` method that cancels the enrollment and sets the cancellation date.

Listing 3.9 `Enrollment` **entity**

```
class Enrollment {
  private Employee employee;
  private Calendar dateOfEnrollment;
  private boolean status;
  private Optional<Calendar> dateOfCancellation;

  public Enrollment(Employee employee, Calendar dateOfEnrollment) {
    this.employee = employee;
    this.dateOfEnrollment = dateOfEnrollment;
    this.status = true;
    this.dateOfCancellation = Optional.empty();
  }

  public void cancel(Calendar dateOfCancellation) {
    this.status = false;
    this.dateOfCancellation = Optional.of(dateOfCancellation);
  }

  // relevant getters
}
```

We'll make an `Offering` have multiple `Enrollment`s instead of a direct
list of employees. We'll also ensure that all changes in an `Enrollment`
happen through the `Offering` that the `Enrollment` belongs to. After all,
we can't allow clients to change enrollments directly. Imagine if a client cancels an enrollment but forgets to update the number of available spots (there's another spot available now that one was
canceled). To ensure that we have no consistency problems, we
make `Offering` an aggregate root and `Enrollment` one of its aggregates.

The `enroll` method (I changed the name of `addEmployee` to `enroll`
because that name makes more sense from this new business angle)
creates a new instance of `Enrollment`, puts it in the list of enrollments,
and decreases the number of available spots. If someone wants to cancel their participation in a course, `Offering` offers the `cancel` method,
which looks up that employee's enrollment, cancels it, and then
makes the spot available again. I won't illustrate the changes in the
`AddEmployeeToOfferingService` class as they are minimal (mostly call
`enroll()` instead of `addEmployee()` and perhaps rename it to `Enroll-
AnEmployeeToOfferingService` to reflect the new domain terms better).

Listing 3.10 `Offering` **as an aggregate root**

```
class Offering {

  private int id;
  private Training training;
  private Calendar date;
  private List<Enrollment> enrollments;        The list of employees is replaced
  private int maximumNumberOfAttendees;        by a list of enrollments.
  private int availableSpots;

  public Offering(
   Training training,
   Calendar date,
   int maximumNumberOfAttendees) {
    // basic constructor
  }                                            Creates an enrollment and
                                               ensures that the offering is in
  public void enroll(Employee employee) {      a consistent state after that
    if(!hasAvailableSpots())
      throw new OfferingIsFullException();

    Calendar now = Calendar.getInstance();
    enrollments.add(new Enrollment(employee, now));
    availableSpots--;
  }                                            Cancels the enrollment and
                                               ensures that the entire
  public void cancel(Employee employee) {      aggregate is consistent
    Enrollment enrollmentToCancel = findEnrollmentOf(employee);
    if(enrollmentToCancel == null)
      throw new EmployeeNotEnrolledException();

    Calendar now = Calendar.getInstance();
    enrollmentToCancel.cancel(now);
                                               Loops through the
    availableSpots++;                          list of enrollments
  }                                            and finds the one
                                               for that employee.
  private Enrollment findEnrollmentOf(Employee employee) {   Returns null
    // loops through the list of enrollments and            otherwise.
    // finds the one for that employee
    // ...
  }
}
```

Note how the `Offering` aggregate root ensures that the entire aggregation is consistent. No client should be able to manipulate enrollments. Again, you can play with your programming language so clients can't use the `Enrollment` entity directly.

Canceling an enrollment may become a service in the future, as it may have more complex consistency checks and validation rules. In that case, the service will ensure that the cancellation is valid and then call the aggregate to propagate the cancellation to the Offering, just as we did with adding an offering.

Figure 3.6 illustrates this aggregate root. Offering is the aggregate root, and Enrollment is an internal domain object. All operations in the offering or its internal domain objects must go through the aggregate root. The design should prevent any modification of internal domain objects.

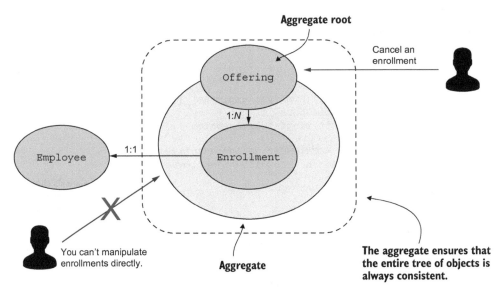

Figure 3.6   An illustration of the Offering aggregate root

Although this is primarily a topic for chapter 6, let me discuss my decision in the   cancel() method. The method finds the enrollment to cancel by looping through the list of Enrollments. In practice, we have to load the entire list of enrollments from the database before finding the one we need. This may not be performant enough, depending on your nonfunctional requirements.

In the case of PeopleGrow!, the list of employees in a training course is small, and the system isn't expected to have an extremely high load. Loading the list of employees shouldn't ever cause performance problems—but you never know. We'll look at this example in chapter 6 when I discuss how to get the best out of your infrastructure without compromising much of your design.

3.6   *Exercises*

Think through the following questions or discuss them with a colleague:

1 Have you ever faced a bug caused by an object's lack of consistency? What was this bug like? How did you fix it?

2 What are the real-world challenges of ensuring that things are correctly consistent and encapsulated?

3 How have you been designing consistency checks and validation mechanisms in your software systems? How much does that approach differ from what's presented in this chapter?

4 Were you aware of the domain-driven design concept of aggregates? Do you see opportunities to apply it in your current project? Where? Why? How?

Summary

- Object consistency is crucial to prevent bugs, reduce coding effort, and ensure smooth maintenance. Consistency should be ensured first in the class, with all of its methods making sure no invalid changes occur.

- Complex business operations may require external validation, which should be handled by services or dedicated validation classes working with the central entity to ensure consistency.

- Avoid creating getters and setters blindly, and reflect on the needs of each method.

- Design aggregate roots in complex entities to ensure the consistency of the entire object graph and prevent clients from updating the internal state of the aggregate.

Managing dependencies

4

This chapter covers

- Reducing the effect of coupling in the class design
- Depending on high-level, more stable code
- Avoiding tightly coupled classes
- Increasing flexibility and testability with dependency injection

In any software system, classes get together to deliver more extensive behavior. For example, a service class may depend on several repositories and entities to do its job. This means the service is coupled to these other classes.

We've discussed the problems of large classes and the advantages of smaller classes. On the one hand, having a class depend on other classes instead of doing everything alone is good. On the other hand, once a class delegates part of its task to another class, it has to "trust" the other class to do its job right. If a developer introduces a bug in an entity, this bug may propagate to the service class and make it break without even touching its code.

That's why you shouldn't randomly add more dependencies to a class. Dependency management or, in simpler words, which classes depend on which classes and whether this is good or bad, is critical when maintaining large software systems.

It's easy to lose control of dependencies. For example, suppose we make a class depend on the details of a dependency. Suddenly, any change in the dependency creates a ripple effect of changes throughout the codebase, increasing the system's complexity and making it harder to maintain over time. Now suppose we make a class depend on many other classes. Besides the code complexity that emerges from the many interactions with the other classes, too many of those classes may change and affect our class. We don't want that.

Managing dependencies is like layering a cake. If you don't do it well, the cake will fall. In this chapter, I talk about patterns that can help you get your dependencies under control.

4.1 Separate high-level and low-level code

Separate code with high-level behavior from low-level implementation code to minimize the effect of changes. High-level code should primarily depend on other high-level code, reducing the potential effects of changes to low-level details. By isolating high-level code, we can create a more modular and adaptable system that is easier to maintain and update over time.

Most business functionalities can be seen from both high- and low-level perspectives. The high-level perspective describes *what* the functionality should do, and the low-level perspective describes *how* it should accomplish the task.

This explicit separation in the code is good for maintenance, especially for complex features and business rules. We want pieces of code that describe only the feature (the high-level code) and other pieces that concretely implement the feature.

There are advantages to following this pattern. First, when maintaining code, starting from the high-level code gives us a quicker understanding of the feature, as the code contains only the "what" and not the "how." We dive into implementing the lower-level details only if we have to. Maintaining code is much easier when it doesn't require reading hundreds of lines before understanding what it does. By hiding details, developers can focus on what's important.

Second, the separation between higher-level and lower-level code allows them to change and evolve separately. For example, we can change the internal details of the lower level without affecting the higher level and vice versa.

Third, higher-level code tends to be more abstract and, consequently, more stable. Therefore, when we make our code always depend on other higher-level code, we are less likely to be affected by a change.

You may have heard of the dependency inversion principle (DIP), which is a name to describe what I just said. This principle states that we should depend on abstractions, not details. Moreover, higher-level and lower-level classes should depend only on abstractions, not other lower-level classes. Although I'm less strict about depending solely on abstractions, separating high-level and low-level concerns is more critical than creating unnecessary abstractions. Some low-level components are stable enough not to require additional abstractions.

4.1.1   Design stable code

When writing higher-level code, we mostly write "stable code," which is good. Interfaces are an example of units of code that are stable over time because they define, in a high-level way, what a component offers the external world. Interfaces don't care about internal implementation details and are a great way to decouple high-level code from low-level code.

Interfaces don't work miracles. Bad interfaces can still be designed: for example, interfaces that aren't stable or leak internal implementation details. We need to design interfaces with stability and information hiding in mind.

4.1.2   Interface discovery

Writing all the high-level code first and implementing the details later is an interesting programming style, which you get better at the more you practice.

There are many advantages to coding this way. Not only is there a clear separation between higher-level and lower-level code, but this approach also prevents you from getting stuck. If you tackle the implementation details in the order they appear, then as soon as a new requirement arises, you have to search for the solution, distracting you from your original focus. By coding the high-level functionality first, you can handle the implementation details later, resulting in a productivity boost.

Coding the high-level interfaces first enables you to explore what the contract of the class should look like and what operations it should offer to its clients. This is a great design tool to ensure that your interfaces stay sharp and to the point and don't contain methods or require information that's not needed.

NOTE Steve Freeman and Nat Pryce's book *Growing Object-Oriented Systems, Guided by Tests* (Addison-Wesley Professional, 2009) brilliantly illustrates how interface discovery can help you build maintainable object-oriented design. This book is worth the read.

4.1.3 When not to separate the higher level from the lower level

Not every feature needs to be separated into higher-level and lower-level code, because not all features in a software system are complex. Mixing the high-level description of what needs to happen with its implementation can be acceptable for more straightforward features. You can encapsulate the implementation details of the higher-level code using private methods, making navigating to the implementation details easier if needed. As always, as soon as you realize complexity is growing, refactor.

The only things I suggest you never mix, regardless of the complexity of the feature, are infrastructure and business code. You don't want your business logic mixed with SQL queries or HTTP calls to get information from a web service. In these cases, you should always have a higher-level interface that describes the "what" and put the implementation details in lower-level classes. I talk more about that in chapter 6.

4.1.4 Example: The messaging job

PeopleGrow! has a background job that runs every 5 seconds and sends messages to users. The code gets unsent messages, retrieves the user's internal ID from their email, sends the message using the internal communicator, and marks the message as sent.

> **Listing 4.1   High-level unit of code for `MessageSender`**

```
public class MessageSender {
  private Bot bot;
  private UserDirectory userDirectory;
  private MessageRepository repository;
  public MessageSender(Bot bot,
   UserDirectory userDirectory,
   MessageRepository repository) {
    this.bot = bot;
    this.userDirectory = userDirectory;
    this.repository = repository;               Loops through all the
  }                                         messages that need to be sent
  public void sendMessages() {
    List<Message> messagesToBeSent = repository.getMessagesToBeSent();
    for(Message messageToBeSent : messagesToBeSent) {
      String userId = userDirectory.
        getAccount(messageToBeSent.getEmail());        Gets the user's ID
      bot.sendPrivateMessage(userId,                   based on their email
        messageToBeSent.getBodyInMarkdown());
      messageToBeSent.markAsSent();                  Sends the message
    }                                                through the bot
  }                       Marks the message as sent
}
interface Bot {
  void sendPrivateMessage(String userId, String messageToBeSent);
}
interface UserDirectory {
  String getAccount(String email);
}
interface MessageRepository {
  List<Message> getMessagesToBeSent();
}
```

Note how high-level this code is. It solely describes what's expected from this job and contains no low-level implementation details of any of these parts. We know that `MessageRepository` returns the list of messages to be sent, but we don't know how. We know that `UserDirectory` gets the user ID based on an email, but we don't know how this is done. The same thing for the `Bot` interface; we know what it does but not how it does it.

Any developer who bumps into this code snippet will understand what this job does. Sure, the developer may not know the implementation details, but do they need to know? You rarely need to know how everything in a business flow works. It's more common that, in maintenance tasks, you find the small part of the flow that you want to change, and you make the change. Imagine how complex software development would be if you had to understand every single detail of the software system before being able to change it.

In figure 4.1, you can see that MessageSender depends on interfaces that are likely to be stable, such as MessageRepository, UserDirectory, and Bot. These interfaces are implemented by low-level code that gets things done. For example, the MessageRepository interface is implemented by the)MessageHibernateRepository class, which uses Hibernate (a Java persistence framework) for database access. The UserDirectory interface is implemented by a CachedLdapServer class that caches the information retrieved by the company's Lightweight Directory Access Protocol (LDAP) server, and Bot is implemented by an HttpBot class that makes an HTTP call to the API. We only know the implementation details once we dive into the lower-level classes.

The implementation details of how the lower-level classes do their jobs are not of concern to MessageSender. It only needs to know that the Bot interface offers a way to send a markdown message to a specific user. The MessageSender interface is decoupled from the implementation details, which is what we want.

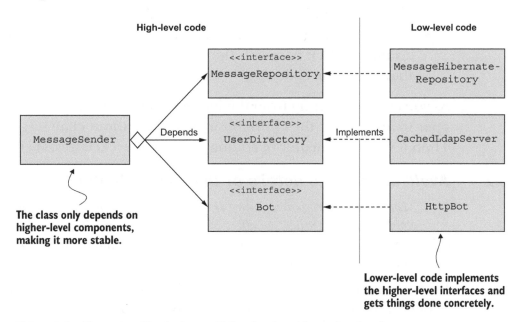

Figure 4.1 The separation between higher-level and lower-level code

In terms of coding, the developer who implemented this class followed the suggestion of implementing the higher-level code first (or, in other words, following a more top-down approach rather than bottom-up). So, they did the following:

1 They started to write the entire `MessageSender` class without caring about the details.

2 At some point, they needed the list of messages to be sent. `MessageRepository` already existed, so they added a new method to the interface.

3 They needed to retrieve the user ID based on the user's email. This was the first time that information was required. They created the `UserDirectory` interface and continued with `MessageSender`.

4 It was time to send the message to the bot. This was also the first time a bot was required, so they wrote the `Bot` interface.

5 Once `MessageSender` was done, they changed their focus to the lower-level classes.

6 They implemented `getMessagesToBeSent()` in the repository.

7 They investigated and learned that the user ID should come from the LDAP server. They found a library to help communicate with the LDAP server and wrote the class.

8 They read the documentation of the chat tool and learned that a simple HTTP post with the message would be enough. Then they wrote the code.

As you can see, starting from the higher-level code allowed the developer to implement the entire business logic without changing focus. Then it was just a matter of coding the lower-level classes. Well done!

4.2 *Avoid coupling to details or things you don't need*

Minimize dependencies on the implementation details of other components to reduce the effect of internal changes. The less you know about how components do their job, the less likely you are to be affected by changes to their implementation.

Rule number one in good dependency management is to never depend on the details of other classes or components. The best way to achieve this is by ensuring that classes don't expose their details in the first place.

Hiding the internal details of classes is crucial for evolving software components independently without worrying about other components. Imagine having to change hundreds of classes in your system just because you performed a refactoring in a single class. This would be time consuming and expensive.

In computer science, this principle is also known as *information hiding*. The idea is to separate what's likely to change from what's not so that other components don't have to be modified too much when we change these parts.

Although it's impossible to hide every detail of a class, we can explicitly design what we expose and what we conceal. Here are some guidelines to help:

- If you change the internal implementation of this class—say, you refactor it—will clients be affected?
- Will this piece of code need frequent changes? If so, can you design it so the code is hidden behind a more stable abstraction, like an interface?
- Is this the minimum information the client needs to know? Less is better.
- Are you unnecessarily exposing implementation details? If the client doesn't need to know, don't reveal it.

In short, you must decide what to expose and what to conceal and reflect on how much changes to the details you expose will affect clients.

4.2.1 *Only require or return classes that you own*

When designing classes or interfaces, it's important to require or return only classes you own, not classes from a framework or third-party library. By a "class you own," I mean a class that belongs to your domain model and over which you have complete control and ownership; for example, an entity, repository, or new data structure you created for this new requirement. By returning only classes you own, you avoid coupling your code to external dependencies, such as a particular library or structure.

The importance of this pattern emerges when you start integrating your code with other modules or third-party libraries. Say you decided to adopt the software development kit (SDK) of the chat tool your company uses internally. If you pass the classes from the chat SDK throughout your entire codebase, you strongly couple your code to it. What happens if the SDK changes? You'll be forced to either never update to the newer SDK or to propagate the change to the entire codebase, which is cumbersome and expensive. A way out of this problem is to create classes that represent the communication with the chat tool from your domain's point of view and let one class in your system handle the conversion between the domain and the chat SDK.

Although the two aforementioned approaches may seem slightly different, they have distinctly different consequences. If the third-party library changes, we only need to propagate the change to the converter class.

We can't avoid coupling entirely, but we can control what our code is coupled to. Be cautious not to overdo it and create excessive layers of indirection or needlessly complex code. In some cases, a third-party class is precisely what's needed, and coupling to it is acceptable. It's up to you to judge how "bad" the coupling is.

> ### The cost of onboarding developers
> Something to keep in mind when creating wrappers or internal libraries and frameworks is that they will have a cost when onboarding a new developer. The developer likely knows how to use a widely used open source library, but they won't know how your unique layer on top of it works. So, make sure your wrapper is simple enough. This idea appears again in chapter 6 when I talk about connecting your design with external infrastructure.

Last but not least, returning classes we own makes the most sense in our domain classes. We don't want our `Invoice` or `Product` classes to be coupled to a data structure from another library we have little control over. However, we don't have to wrap every single class of every single framework in our tech stack. On the contrary: it's often better to embrace the framework's way of doing things. I have a rule of thumb that I never create wrappers around the major frameworks I picked for the project's tech stack.

For example, if I choose Spring Boot as my framework of choice, I don't wrap its classes so that later, I can replace Spring with another framework. I do my best not to let Spring Boot get spread over my domain classes, but I don't wrap the controller classes just so my controller becomes independent from Spring. Spring also offers facilities to implement repository classes. If you use it, your repositories may be coupled to some of Spring's functionalities and not a framework-independent class, but this shouldn't be a problem.

I used a Java framework as an example, but the same is true when you pick similar frameworks in other languages. If you choose Ruby on Rails or ASP.NET Core, embrace the framework unless you have excellent reasons not to.

4.2.2 *Example: Replacing the HTTP bot with the chat SDK*

The internal communication system used by the company now offers an SDK for the integration that PeopleGrow! can use. This means a better SDK implementation can replace HttpBot. Given that the Bot interface clearly defines what a bot needs to implement (high-level code), all we need to do is implement a new class that implements this interface (low-level code).

The SDK offers a ChatBotV1 class with a writeMessage method that receives a BotMessage (a class that's part of the SDK) as a parameter. Given that we don't own this class, we don't let it go outside the low-level implementation of the new SDKBot class we're about to implement.

Listing 4.2 Implementation of SDKBot

```
class SDKBot implements Bot {                                    Instantiates the
  public void sendPrivateMessage(String userId, String msg) {   chatbot class
    var chatBot = new ChatBotV1();              <──────────      from the SDK
    var message = new BotMessage(userId, msg);  <──────
    chatBot.writeMessage(message);  <──                   Composes the BotMessage,
  }                         Sends the message to the bot via the   also part of the SDK
}                           SDK's provided writeMessage() method
```

In no situation should we return instances of BotMessage to other parts of the code. This way, the rest of the codebase is fully decoupled from the library, allowing us to change the implementation in the future.

You may have noticed that we instantiate `ChatBotV1` directly in `sendPrivateMessage`. A better way to do this would be to inject it into the `SDKBot` class. We talk about dependency injection later in this chapter.

4.2.3   *Don't give clients more than they need*

In information systems, it's common to reuse the same domain entities in different parts of the application. The same entity retrieved from a repository is used by the service and then sent back to the client that requested it (after, say, being serialized to JSON). We do this because it's too easy to reuse an existing class even if the client's needs differ.

I'll focus on the example of the same entity being shared across different layers of the application, as it's the most common type of reuse I see. Figure 4.2 illustrates this.

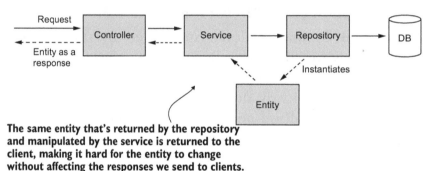

The same entity that's returned by the repository and manipulated by the service is returned to the client, making it hard for the entity to change without affecting the responses we send to clients.

Figure 4.2   The same entity is used across different layers, creating some undesired coupling.

Giving clients the entire entity, not only what they need, has disadvantages. First, any change in the entity is propagated to the client. Could this change break the client? There may also be security implications. What if we add a field the client shouldn't see or know about? The worst part is that it's hard for the developer to do an impact analysis on the fly and identify whether the change to the entity will affect clients.

A great solution to this issue is to decouple the entity from what the clients requested. We can achieve this by creating a more specific data structure representing the client's needs and then converting the entity to this data structure before sending it to the client. This way, we can change the entity without worrying about how it will affect clients.

What we are doing here is *abstracting* the information. We are used to abstract behavior, but we can also abstract information!

4.2.4   *Example: The offering list*

PeopleGrow! has a page in the web system that lists all the current offerings, the number of enrollments, and the number of available spots. The `Offering` entity contains all this information. However, if we return this entire entity to the frontend client, we'll return too much information it doesn't need. For example, this page doesn't need the names of the enrolled employees. In some architectures, returning this list of employees may even have a performance cost as it requires more queries to the database.

Listing 4.3   `Offering` class

```
class Offering {
  private int id;
  private Training training;
  private Calendar date;
  private Set<Employee> employees;
  private int maximumNumberOfAttendants;
  private int numberOfAvailableSpots;
  // relevant constructors, getters, and setters
}
```

Instead of returning the full-blown entity, we'll create a data structure that holds only the information the client needs. The `Offering-Summary` class contains only the title, date, number of enrollments, and total number of spots. This class is constructed after the main entity.

Listing 4.4   `OfferingSummary` class

```
class OfferingSummary {
  private int id;
  private String training;
  private Calendar date;
  private int numberOfEnrollments;
  private int maximumNumberOfAttendants;
  // relevant constructors and getters
}
```

We only need to build `OfferingSummary` based on the `Offering` entity. The question is where to put this code. I've seen developers put it in different places, but these are the best two:

- A method `OfferingSummary toSummary()` inside the `Offering` entity. This ensures that the conversion logic stays inside the entity.
- A static method `OfferingSummary convert(Offering offering)` in the `OfferingSummary` class. This way, the conversion logic becomes closer to the data structure, freeing the entity from knowing that this data structure exists.

I prefer the second option as I like my domain entities to be agnostic regarding the clients' needs. But the first one is also OK and won't give you complicated maintenance challenges.

4.3 *Break down classes that depend on too many other classes*

Break down classes with too many dependencies to limit the scope of potential changes. This pattern improves code maintainability and flexibility, allowing your system to better adapt to changing requirements.

Units of code should be small in all dimensions, including dependencies. If a class depends on 10 other classes, it may indicate a design problem and cause maintenance issues in the future.

As features grow more complex, dependency numbers increase. When we're adding functionality to an existing feature, there are two primary options (figure 4.3). One is to expand the current code unit, which doesn't add dependencies but increases complexity, as mentioned in chapter 2. The other option is to create a new class and link it to the existing one, which increases coupling without increasing the original feature's complexity.

When a class starts to depend on many other classes, and they themselves have grown, consider breaking the cycle. Explore alternatives, including those that follow.

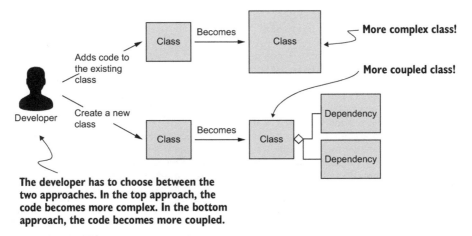

The developer has to choose between the two approaches. In the top approach, the code becomes more complex. In the bottom approach, the code becomes more coupled.

Figure 4.3 Add code to the same class or create a new class? Both decisions have advantages and disadvantages.

4.3.1 *Example: Breaking down the MessageSender service*

Consider the `MessageSender` service in PeopleGrow!. It depends on three classes:

- `UserDirectory`—Communicates with the user directory, obtaining user IDs from emails
- `Bot`—Sends messages to users via the company's internal chat system
- `MessageRepository`—Retrieves messages to be sent at a specific time

Now imagine a new request to deliver messages via email if the user prefers. We find the existing `EmailSender` class and add it as the fourth dependency. A fifth dependency, `UserPreferences`, is introduced to obtain user preferences.

Listing 4.5   Sending a message by email

```
public class MessageSender {
  private Bot bot;
  private UserDirectory userDirectory;
  private MessageRepository repository;
  private EmailSender emailSender;          Adds new dependencies
  private UserPreferences userPrefs;        to MessageServer
  public MessageSender(Bot bot,
    UserDirectory userDirectory,
    MessageRepository repository,
```

```
    EmailSender emailSender,
    UserPreferences userPrefs) {
     this.bot = bot;
     this.userDirectory = userDirectory;
     this.repository = repository;
     this.emailSender = emailSender;
     this.userPrefs = userPrefs;
   }
   public void sendMessages() {
     List<Message> messagesToBeSent = repository.getMessagesToBeSent();
     for(Message messageToBeSent : messagesToBeSent) {
       String userId = userDirectory.getAccount(messageToBeSent.getEmail());
       bot.sendPrivateMessage(userId, messageToBeSent.getBodyInMarkdown());
       if(userPrefs.sendViaEmail(messageToBeSent.getEmail())) {         ◄─┐
         emailSender.sendMessage(messageToBeSent);
       }
       // mark the message as sent
       messageToBeSent.markAsSent();
     }
   }
}
```
These two dependencies are used to decide whether to send a copy of the message to the user's email.

A class that was previously dependent on three classes now depends on five. This is not good. We should break down this class and move some dependencies to regain control.

For instance, the `Bot` interface could be changed from `sendPrivate-Message(user id, markdown message)` to `sendPrivateMessage(Message)`, because the `Message` object includes the user's email and the message. This change may necessitate updates to the code but may be manageable if the bot isn't widely used.

If modifying an existing interface is costly, try creating a wrapper class that groups dependencies, especially if it can be given a meaningful domain name. For example, a `MessageBot` class can combine the responsibilities of obtaining the user ID and sending the message. This class has a single `send()` method that takes a `Message` object and calls `UserDirectory` and `Bot`.

Listing 4.6   `MessageBot` class

```
public class MessageBot {
  private Bot bot;
  private UserDirectory userDirectory;
  public MessageBot(Bot bot,
    UserDirectory userDirectory) {        ◄─┘
     this.bot = bot;
     this.userDirectory = userDirectory;
  }
  public void send(Message msg) {          ◄─┐
```
This class depends on UserDirectory and Bot.

It uses both to send the message to the bot, the same way as in MessageSender.

```
    String userId = userDirectory.getAccount(msg.getEmail());
    bot.sendPrivateMessage(userId, msg.getBodyInMarkdown());
    }
  }
}
```

Introducing this new class has benefits: doing so reduces client coupling by replacing `Bot` and `UserDirectory` in `MessageSender` with `Message-Bot`, simplifying the `Bot` interface. The drawback is managing an additional class in the code.

The "grouping dependencies" tactic can also apply to `UserPreferences` and `EmailSender`. `EmailSender` can depend on `UserPreferences` to verify user email preferences, reducing the dependency count by one more. Compare the dependencies in `MessageSender` in figures 4.4 (before) and 4.5 (after).

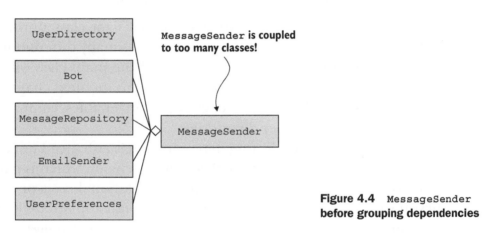

Figure 4.4 `MessageSender` **before grouping dependencies**

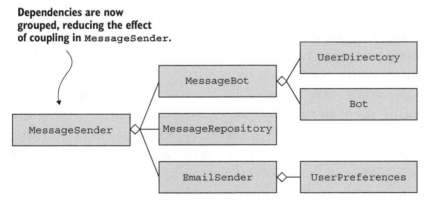

Figure 4.5 `MessageSender` **after grouping dependencies**

> ## Indirect coupling
>
> In the example, `MessageSender` depends on `MessageBot`, which relies on `UserDirectory` and `Bot`. Although `MessageSender` doesn't directly depend on `UserDirectory` and `Bot`, it has indirect dependencies. Although also critical, indirect coupling is less concerning than direct coupling. If the `Bot` class changes, the modification won't affect `MessageSender` because it doesn't directly use the bot. As long as `MessageBot` effectively encapsulates the `Bot` usage, changes are unlikely to propagate beyond `MessageBot`.

4.4   *Inject dependencies, aka dependency injection*

Enable dependency injection in components to increase flexibility and testability. By allowing dependencies to be injected, components become more modular and can be easily tested in isolation.

Passing different concrete implementations to a class during run time gives a design flexibility. We can create as many different implementations of an interface as we want, and the main class will work just fine. We explore extensible abstractions in the next chapter; for now, understand that dependency injection enables compatibility with various bots and user directories.

Another benefit of injecting dependencies is enhanced testability. Developers can easily inject mocked dependencies, which is particularly useful when dependencies have computational costs or extend beyond the application. I won't discuss design for testability here (see my other book, *Effective Software Testing: A Developer's Guide:* www.manning.com/books/effective-software-testing), but you get this for free if your classes allow dependencies to be injected.

The best part is that the implementation is simple. We only need to create constructors that receive the class's dependencies instead of instantiating them directly.

There are few benefits in hardcoding dependencies and not allowing them to be injected. In the past, teams working on highly performant applications avoided dependency injection due to its computational costs. These concerns are largely outdated. Dependency injection frameworks are optimized for performance, and virtual machines have improved, handling numerous short-lived object allocations. Unless you're working at the scale of Google or

Facebook, dependency injection performance costs are unlikely to be a problem.

Another common argument against dependency injection was that using static methods was a way to simplify the dependency graph, but this is misleading. Coupling still exists, and now we have less control over it. When dependencies are injected through constructors, developers can easily see a class's dependencies. Identifying dependencies becomes difficult with static methods, as they're dispersed throughout the class's source code.

Interestingly, dependency injection is a typical pattern nowadays because most frameworks, such as Spring Boot and ASP.NET Core, support it.

4.4.1   Avoid static methods for operations that change the state

Static methods can't be replaced at run time, making the design inflexible and hindering testing. Using static methods as a design pattern can lead to a chaotic, hard-to-maintain system.

The problem with using static methods as a design pattern is that the design quickly becomes a big ball of mud. I've seen systems that performed database access inside static methods. For a static method to call the database, it needs an active connection. Because static methods can call only static methods, we need a static method that returns the active connection. To create a connection, we need all the database information. There we go: another static method to return the database configuration. Before we know it, we are stuck with a set of methods that can't be injected.

Another way to reason about what can be static and what can't is to look at how "pure" the operation is. A simple utility method that receives a string and returns the number of commas in that string is an example of a pure operation. It doesn't depend on many other classes, and, more importantly, it doesn't depend on any external resources. It's often okey for pure functions to be static methods, as we rarely have to replace them during production or testing.

Conversely, the methods in the earlier service class examples are impure functions. They change the system state (for example, by persisting new information into the database) and may yield different results even with the same input. Such classes and operations shouldn't be static.

4.4.2   *Always inject collaborators: Everything else is optional*

Classes in information systems often implement different behaviors and collaborate with other classes to deliver complex features. For example, the MessageSender class we discussed earlier in this chapter relies on Bot, UserDirectory, and MessageRepository as collaborators, and each is responsible for a different aspect of the "sending messages to users" feature.

Collaborators should always be injected. After all, collaborators are the dependencies we may want to change in the future (say, change to a new bot) or mock during testing (like UserDirectory, because we shouldn't require an entire LDAP server to be available during testing).

However, not all dependencies are collaborators. A class may use entities or other data structures representing information. These aren't typically injected. It's more common for classes or services to use repositories or factories to instantiate them rather than receive them from clients. If clients have the entity in their hands, it's expected that they pass it to other classes via the parameters of a method.

4.4.3   *Strategies to instantiate the class together with its dependencies*

A pragmatic question around dependency injection is how to instantiate such a deep graph of dependencies. Dependency injection frameworks remove all the cumbersome work of instantiating complex dependency graphs for you. My favorite option has always been relying on a dependency injection framework such as Spring, Guice, or whatever is available in your programming language. In larger applications, you are likely using a framework to support you in this endeavor, such as Spring or ASP.NET MVC, and a dependency injection framework comes out of the box.

Some developers think that hiding this work from us makes us create even more complex dependency graphs. After all, if we had to instantiate classes manually, we'd see all the work required and redesign our code to simplify the graph. Although I agree with that, there are other ways to get the same type of information that don't require doing a lot of manual work.

That being said, I don't use dependency injection frameworks for more straightforward applications. I have built a lot of small command-line tools in recent years. In these cases, I prefer factory classes that instantiate my dependency graph rather than configuring a dependency injection framework.

Using a dependency injection framework is, in the end, a decision full of trade-offs. Pick one, get all the benefits of your chosen option, and ensure that the downsides are controlled.

4.4.4 *Example: Dependency injection in MessageSender and collaborators*

The MessageSender class in PeopleGrow! was born with the idea of dependency injection in mind, so all of its dependencies are injected through the constructor. If we take the idea of dependency injection further, the dependencies of MessageSender also require their own dependencies to be injected via the constructor.

Figure 4.6 illustrates the dependency graph when we instantiate MessageSender. Luckily, PeopleGrow! uses dependency injection, so the dependencies are automatically injected whenever we need to use MessageSender.

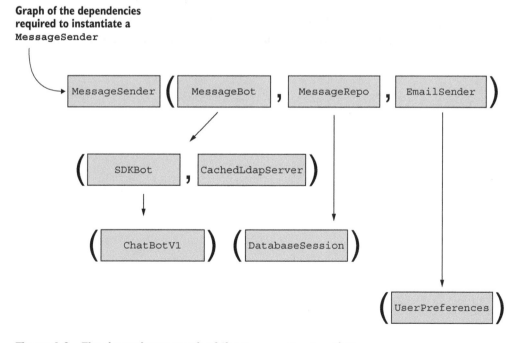

Figure 4.6   The dependency graph of the MessageSender **class**

4.5   *Exercises*

Think through the following questions or discuss them with a colleague:

1 Have you ever suffered from a software system that didn't manage its dependencies properly? What were the consequences? What did you do, if anything?
2 How often do you separate high-level code from low-level code? Do you (now) see advantages in doing so?
3 Some developers don't like using dependency injection frameworks. What's your opinion about it?

Summary

- Minimizing how much a class knows of its dependencies is essential to reduce the effect of changes in the dependencies.
- Separate high-level and low-level code, and depend on more stable abstractions. Avoid excessive dependencies, and identify opportunities for better abstractions.
- Use dependency injection to increase flexibility and simplify testing. Classes should allow collaborators to be injected.

Designing good abstractions

This chapter covers
- Understanding abstractions
- Adding abstractions in code
- Keeping abstractions simple

Good abstractions allow us to add new functionality to a system without constantly changing existing code. For example, think of a bookstore with a range of discounts like "Buy three books, get one free," "45% off during Christmas," and "Buy five e-books, get one printed copy free." The marketing team proposes new discounts regularly, so the development team needs an easy way to add them to the code. A well-designed software system will have abstractions in place so developers can add new discounts with minimal effort.

It's difficult to define what abstractions are in one sentence, so I'll use a few:

- They describe a concept, functionality, or process in a way that clients can understand without knowing the underlying mechanisms.
- They focus on essential characteristics and ignore nonessential ones.
- Abstractions don't care (and don't know) about their concrete implementations.

Abstractions work well with extension points. An extension point enables developers to extend or modify the system's functionality. In the bookstore, an extension point would allow developers to plug in or unplug whatever discounts should be applied for a given basket.

Edsger Dijkstra, a remarkable computer scientist, once said, "Being abstract is something profoundly different from being vague. The purpose of abstraction is not to be vague but to create a new semantic level in which one can be absolutely precise."

Designing abstractions is the most fun part of working on object-oriented systems. It involves identifying common characteristics among existing and future business rules or functionalities and expressing them in abstract terms.

Abstractions and extension points are a way to achieve modularity and flexibility in software design, as they allow different parts of a system to evolve independently of each other. However, creating effective abstractions can be challenging. A wrong abstraction can be worse than not having one. To truly facilitate system evolution, we must go beyond simply creating interfaces for things. Abstractions must be carefully planned and thought through.

Creating good abstractions is like designing a perfect puzzle whose pieces fit together nicely. In this chapter, I discuss patterns that can help you understand when it's time for an abstraction, how to design good and simple abstractions, and when not to use them.

5.1   Design abstractions and extension points

Create abstractions and extension points in your system to accommodate variability and simplify adding new functionality. They improve maintainability and flexibility while minimizing the need to rewrite existing code.

Abstractions and extension points enable us to easily plug new features or variations of existing features into a software system. A software system without them forces developers to make existing code more complex whenever a new feature comes in.

It's common to see classes full of `if` statements, each block handling a different variation of a feature, or classes with several blocks of code, each handling one piece of the functionality. Without proper abstractions, the only way to extend a feature is to write more code into existing classes or methods, making them even more complex.

As we've discussed, having a class with a couple of `ifs` or blocks of code isn't problematic. The problem appears once this number explodes. I once saw a class with around 40 `if` blocks, one for each feature variation; each block contained around 20 lines of code, and all the blocks had many similarities. As you can imagine, the class had no tests, and no engineers wanted to maintain it. A brave engineer eventually refactored the class. Their solution was to create an interface that each variant implemented. They then implemented something similar to the Template Method design pattern, reducing most duplicated code across variants. Life was much better afterward.

I won't dive into how to implement abstractions or teach design patterns, as the existing literature is extensive. Instead, I'll talk about when to add an abstraction and pitfalls to pay attention to.

5.1.1 Identifying the need for an abstraction

You shouldn't introduce a new abstraction because "it looks cool." After all, abstractions add flexibility but also complexity to the code. There must be a reason for you to create one.

When is it a good idea to introduce an abstraction? Some of my rules of thumb are as follows:

- Features that require lots of variations. This way, whenever a new variation appears, all you need to do is to create yet another implementation of the abstraction.
- Features that require flexibility in terms of composability. If a feature has dozens of variations and you may assemble a different combination for each client, then having an abstraction helps you combine variations without much extra code.

- Places where you expect changes in the future. If you know that parts of the feature will likely change, you can do yourself a favor and facilitate this change through good design.
- Decisions or code you want to hide from the rest of the system. You can use abstractions to prevent details from leaking to other parts of the code. For example, you should hide database access logic from your domain model. You can do that by introducing an interface that's ignorant of the details.

You may have other reasons to introduce an abstraction. This list is certainly non-exhaustive. Analyze the tradeoffs and see if the extra cost that abstractions bring to the code is worth it.

5.1.2   *Designing an extension point*

Sometimes, having clients use the newly created abstraction directly is enough. When clients depend on the abstraction rather than the concrete implementation, they are decoupled from details that may change. That helps us easily replace one concrete implementation for another without changing a single line in the client's code. For example, recall the Bot interface we created in chapter 4 and that MessageSender used. Depending on the interface rather than the direct HttpBot allowed us to change the bot to SDKBot without any changes in MessageSender itself.

However, in other cases, we design abstractions to provide flexibility and variability to a feature. Consider the bookstore from the beginning of this chapter. The abstraction Discount was created to apply many discounts in the customer's basket. The abstraction isn't enough in this case. We need a mechanism to plug as many varied discount rules as possible into the customer's basket and have them calculate the final price.

Designing an extension point (or not) involves identifying how the abstraction should be used in the wild. You should not only design the abstraction but also put yourself in the shoes of those who will use it.

Extension points are prevalent in open source libraries. Think of any framework you use, such as Spring or ASP. NET MVC. These frameworks provide lots of extension points so that you can customize them. Spring allows you to define different security filters to define your own security rules. These are nothing but extension points.

In business applications, although less commonly than in frameworks, you see them used in features requiring great flexibility; for example, calculating the final price of the customer's basket after going through complex rules, calculating an employee's salary based on many different salary components or rules based on their location, or calculating how much tax to pay for a given invoice based on the types of products sold.

5.1.3   *Attributes of good abstractions*

Designing good abstractions is an art. What does a good abstraction look like?

A good abstraction separates the "what" from the "how." In other words, good abstractions focus on what they should do but know nothing about how it's done. Good abstractions make you, the developer, not care about concrete implementations. You read the code that uses the abstraction, and that's enough for you to know what's going on.

Good abstractions define a clear contract that clients can rely on. They make it clear to clients what their preconditions are and what they promise to deliver. The contracts of a good abstraction are also as lean as possible. They don't expect anything more from clients than the precise data they require to get the job done, and they don't return more than what the clients need.

Once you have a suitable abstraction, writing the different concrete implementations should be easy. You shouldn't need to read lots of documentation or spend hours figuring out what's right and wrong. Good abstractions lead you the correct way from the very beginning. That said, good abstractions are well documented, and developers can learn everything about them without bothering other team developers.

A good abstraction is easy for clients to use. With a few lines of code, you should get the most out of the abstraction. You shouldn't need hundreds of lines of code or have to meet complex requirements to use it. Good abstractions are straightforward.

A good abstraction doesn't force extension points to change whenever it changes or evolves. A good abstraction is, in fact, stable and doesn't change much. That's why coupling to an abstraction is less of a problem than coupling to a more unstable concrete implementation.

Finally, a good abstraction allows us to plug and unplug concrete implementations without requiring any changes in the code. Good abstractions allow developers to mix and match different concrete implementations to compose more complex behavior in very complex features.

5.1.4   *Learn from your abstractions*

Designing abstractions and extension points is not an exact science, and even established frameworks sometimes need to evolve their APIs over time. So, it's natural to expect changes in your code as well.

You should continuously refine abstractions and extension points based on real-world usage. Although valuable for accommodating variability and simplifying code changes, abstractions require ongoing improvement to meet evolving needs. Observe how they are used throughout the software system. Learn from the clients. Listen to the developers. And then improve the abstractions.

The challenge is that you can't keep changing your abstractions and interfaces, as doing so can cause breaking changes in everything that depends on them. Maybe the abstraction you are changing isn't used much, and you can afford to change code everywhere. In other cases, you should consider keeping backward compatibility. Changing abstractions safely is a complex software engineering task that can even be considered an open problem, and I won't dive into it.

5.1.5   *Learn about abstractions*

One valuable resource for learning more about abstractions and how to design extension points is the 1994 book *Design Patterns* by the Gang of Four (Erich Gamma, Richard Helm, Ralph Johnson, and John Vlissides; Addison-Wesley Professional). Many of these patterns involve creating extension points for different parts of the system. These patterns can provide a range of ideas for designing extension points. I strongly recommend studying the following design patterns, especially if you're working on enterprise systems: Strategy, State, Chain of Responsibility, Decorator, Template Method, and Command. Although some may not apply directly to your programming language or framework of choice, you can still learn much from them.

Another excellent resource is to examine the design of open source frameworks. Look closely at your favorite framework to see how it designs extension points. Dive deep into the source code. Exploring the source code of frameworks like Spring can teach you a lot about creating extensible software systems.

5.1.6 *Abstractions and coupling*

In chapter 4, we discussed dependency management and the challenges that high coupling brings to design. There, I also said that designing stable code is a good practice.

Dependency management and designing good abstractions work together. A good abstraction tends to be stable. This means being coupled to an abstraction is less of a problem, as it's less likely to change and, consequently, force other classes to change.

5.1.7 *Example: Giving badges to employees*

PeopleGrow! gives badges to employees who take trainings. Like any gamified system, PeopleGrow! has many badges, and the rules to get one range from simple to complex.

The initial implementation of the badge system is shown in listing 5.1. The `BadgeGiver` class has a `give()` method that receives `Employee`. The implementation goes rule by rule; if employees satisfy that rule, they win the badge. `Badge` is a simple enum that lists the available badges.

As you can see, all the badge-assigning rules are implemented in a single class. A developer has attempted to organize the code: rules are grouped in different private methods, and code comments separate different rules.

Listing 5.1   First implementation of `BadgeGiver`

```java
class BadgeGiver {
  public void give(Employee employee) {         ⟵  Applies all types of different badge-
    perTraining(employee);                         assigning rules: per type of training
    perQuantity(employee);                         and quantity
  }
  private boolean perTraining(Employee employee) {
    TrainingsTaken trainingsTaken = employee.getTrainingsTaken();
    // you get a badge if you did quality-related trainings   ⟵  Each specific
    if(trainingsTaken.has("TESTING") &&                          badge comes
      trainingsTaken.has("CODE QUALITY")) {                      with code
      assign(employee, Badge.QUALITY_HERO);                      comments
    }                                                            to improve
    // you get a badge if you took all the security trainings   legibility.
    if(trainingsTaken.has("SECURITY 101") &&
      trainingsTaken.has("SECURITY FOR MOBILE DEVS")) {
      assign(employee, Badge.SECURITY_COP);
    }                                               The implementation of this
    // ... and many more ...                        method is similar in structure
  }                                                  to the previous one.
  private void perQuantity(Employee employee) {  ⟵
    TrainingsTaken trainingsTaken = employee.getTrainingsTaken();
    if(trainingsTaken.totalTrainings() >= 5) {
      assign(employee, Badge.FIVE_TRAININGS);
    }
    if(trainingsTaken.totalTrainings() >= 10) {
      assign(employee, Badge.TEN_TRAININGS);
    }
    if(trainingsTaken.trainingsInPast3Months() >= 3) {
      assign(employee, Badge.ON_FIRE);
    }
  }
  private void assign(Employee employee, Badge badge) {
    employee.winBadge(badge);
  }
}
```

Let's try a more straightforward design before going for more complex solutions. We can try a pattern we've seen before: breaking a complex class into a few smaller ones.

Let's see what happens if we move the groups of badge rules to different classes. The new `BadgesForTrainings` and `BadgesForQuantity` classes contain just the rules related to their groups of badges. If a new group of badges emerges, we create a new class. `BadgeGiver` now coordinates the work.

Listing 5.2   Groups of badges in different classes

```
class BadgeGiver {
  public void give(Employee employee) {          ◁──┤ BadgeGiver coordinates the
    new BadgesForTrainings().give(employee);            work with the new classes.
    new BadgesForQuantity().give(employee);
  }
}
                                                       The BadgesForTrainings class contains only
                                                       the rules related to badges that employees
class BadgesForTrainings {                        ◁──┤ get if they take specific training courses.
  public void give(Employee employee) {
    // same code for badges for trainings as before
  }                                                    The BadgesForQuantity class
}                                                      contains only rules related
class BadgesForQuantity {                         ◁──  to badges if employees take
  public void give(Employee employee) {               a specific number of training
    // same code for badges for quantity as before    courses.
  }
}
```

The new implementation is more straightforward due to smaller classes, but it's not a suitable final implementation for two reasons. First, the internal implementation of the new classes, BadgesForTrainings and BadgesForQuantity, is repetitive and will continue to grow whenever a new badge becomes available. Second, creating a new group of badges requires modifying BadgeGiver. Although this is a minor issue, improving it can aid in future maintenance.

The first step in improving the implementation is identifying the common behavior we want to abstract: deciding whether a badge must be given to an employee. We can create a BadgeRule interface that generically represents all the rules determining whether a badge should be assigned.

BadgeRule requires two methods from its concrete implementations: give() and badgeToGive(). The first determines whether an employee deserves a badge, and the second returns the badge that should be given.

Listing 5.3   BadgeRule interface

```
interface BadgeRule {
  boolean give(Employee employee);
  Badge badgeToGive();
}
```

We can now implement the different rules, each in its own class. The following listing shows the implementation of three of these rules. All the classes implement the `BadgeRule` abstraction.

Listing 5.4 A few implementations of `BadgeRule`

```
class QualityHero implements BadgeRule {
  public boolean give(Employee employee) {
    TrainingsTaken trainingsTaken = employee.getTrainingsTaken();
    return trainingsTaken.has("TESTING") &&
      trainingsTaken.has("CODE QUALITY"));
  }
  public Badge badgeToGive() {
    return Badge.QUALITY_HERO;
  }
}
class SecurityCop implements BadgeRule {
  public boolean give(Employee employee) {
    TrainingsTaken trainingsTaken = employee.getTrainingsTaken();
    return trainingsTaken.has("SECURITY 101") &&
      trainingsTaken.has("SECURITY FOR MOBILE DEVS"))
  }
  public Badge badgeToGive() {
    return Badge.SECURITY_COP;
  }
}
class FiveTrainings implements BadgeRule {
  public boolean give(Employee employee) {
    TrainingsTaken trainingsTaken = employee.getTrainingsTaken();
    return trainingsTaken.totalTrainings() >= 5;
  }
  public Badge badgeToGive() {
    return Badge.FIVE_TRAININGS;
  }
}
// ... same for the 10 trainings and On Fire badges
```

The QualityHero class checks whether the employee took the two quality-related trainings.

The SecurityCop class checks whether the employee took the security trainings.

The FiveTrainings class checks whether the number of trainings the employee took is greater than 5.

Now that we have a proper abstraction to represent the badge rules, we make `BadgeGiver` depend on the abstraction, not the concrete implementations. We do this by receiving a list of `BadgeRule`s—say, via the constructor. The `give()` method loops through all the rules, checks whether a badge should be given to an employee, and if so, gives the badge.

`BadgeGiver` can work with any new badge we create, as long as the rule implements the `BadgeRule` interface.

Listing 5.5   `BadgeGiver`, **which depends on** `BadgeRule`

```
class BadgeGiver {
  private final List<BadgeRule> rules;
  public BadgeGiver(List<BadgeRule> rules) {        The constructor receives
    this.rules = rules;                             a list of badge rules.
  }
  public void give(Employee employee) {             Loops through all the rules to see whether
    for(BadgeRule rule : rules) {                   the employee deserves that badge
      if(rule.give(employee)) {
        employee.winBadge(rule.badgeToGive());
      }
    }
  }
}
```

Figure 5.1 illustrates what our design looks like now. `BadgeRule` is an abstraction, and badges implement it. Badges are then plugged into `BadgeGiver`, which processes them all.

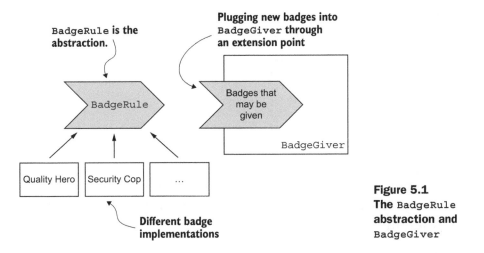

Figure 5.1
The `BadgeRule`
abstraction and
`BadgeGiver`

With this new design, we have reached our first goal: we don't have to change `BadgeGiver` if a new badge emerges. Instead, we implement a new `BadgeRule`.

The next problem to solve is avoiding the explosion of classes. With this design, we need a new class for a badge, even if the badge is similar to an existing one. For example, the badges we give if an employee takes the quality- and the security-related trainings are very similar. The only difference is the training courses we look for—and the same for the badges we give based on quantity. There's a lot of code duplication happening. We'll improve this after we discuss another pattern: generalizing business rules.

Another decision we made in this code was to create the Trainings-Taken class. Note how the method employee.getTrainingsTaken() returns not a simple list of trainings but rather a TrainingsTaken class. This class is a wrapper on top of the list of training courses that encapsulates complex query logic clients may ask for, such as whether a course was taken or how many training courses a person took in the past three months. The following listing illustrates its implementation.

Listing 5.6   TrainingsTaken class

```
class TrainingsTaken {
  private final List<Training> trainings;
  public TrainingsTaken(List<Training> trainings) {      ⟵┐  The class contains the list
    this.trainings = trainings;                              of training courses taken
  }                                                          by the employee.
  public boolean has(String trainingName) {      ⟵┐
    ... find whether the training is in the list of trainings ...    Methods
  }                                                                   encapsulate
  public int totalTrainings() {                                       the query
    ... return the number of completed trainings ...                  logic to
  }                                                                    simplify the
  public int trainingsInPast3Months() {                               clients.
    ... return the number of completed
    ... trainings in the past 3 months
  }
}
```

Creating classes on top of lists of objects is something I suggest doing, especially if you expect clients to query this list in multiple different ways.

5.2   *Generalize important business rules*

Generalize business logic to create multiple variants of the same rule without introducing unnecessary complexity or duplication. This approach facilitates the creation of flexible and scalable code that can adapt to changing requirements and improves code reuse by eliminating redundant code.

Sometimes we must apply the same business rule in different contexts with varying concrete values. Without a proper abstraction, developers may duplicate the original code to account for these slight differences.

If we go back to our bookstore example, suppose a specific discount is based on the authors of the books the customer is buying. For example, if the customer buys books by Kent Beck and Martin Fowler, renowned software engineering authors, they get a discount. They also get a discount if they buy books by Tolkien and Rowling (two of my favorite fiction authors). Now suppose the bookstore has 50 or 60 discounts based on different combinations of authors.

A very naive approach to implement this would be to write a series of `if` statements, each checking whether the authors match the customer's books and, if so, applying the discount. Note how these `if` statements would pertain to the same business rule but with slight variations. Whenever a new discount was added, the developer would copy and modify the business rule, which is not maintainable.

We should identify the general business rule and create an abstraction to solve this issue. Each concrete implementation of this discount is a different instance of the generic business rule but with concrete values.

In essence, this pattern isn't that different from the previous one. Both are about identifying the right abstractions to enable us to evolve the software system with minimal effort. In my experience, it's easier for developers to create extension points or abstractions that resemble different strategies, such as different ways of calculating discounts. Generalizing business rules is more challenging, so I have a dedicated pattern, which I discuss next.

5.2.1   *Separate the concrete data from the generalized business rule*

The main challenge around generalizing business rules is related to data. In most information systems, business related data comes from a database. Mixing business rules and data retrieval concerns without a proper design is easy, but doing so leads to code that is complex and hard to follow. Figure 5.2 illustrates.

Modifying and adding new features becomes challenging when we mix data retrieval and business logic in our code. The code becomes too specialized for one rule, making it challenging to add new variations or enhance its flexibility. In these situations, it's better to segregate the code that fetches data from the code that executes the business logic, just as we did before.

The code is a mix of logic and data retrieval from different sources: in this case, from two different databases and an external webservice.

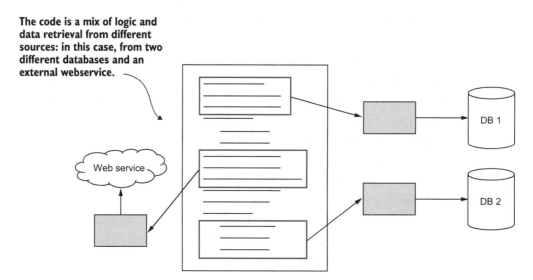

Figure 5.2   Code that mixes business logic and data retrieval quickly becomes messy, hard to maintain, and hard to test.

When generalizing business logic, you should avoid tying it to specific data. Instead, ensure that the abstraction depends not on specific values but rather on generic ones. For example, instead of having "JK Rowling" and "Tolkien" hardcoded in the code, the generalized business logic should deal with a list of authors' names, whoever those authors are.

There are many different ways to implement this approach. Some are manual, others are fancier. For example, having one class that implements the generalized business rule and receives the data through its constructor and another class that's responsible for retrieving the data (via a repository) and instantiating the generic business rule with the concrete data is often a good-enough solution.

The advantage of a simplistic *glue code* is that it's easy to understand and evolve. But the disadvantage is that it can become complex quickly when new discount types emerge.

Deciding how far you should go when designing abstractions is a challenge. As always, there are no rights and wrongs, just different design decisions with different advantages and tradeoffs. Should you go for the most flexible solution immediately or start simple? We'll talk more about this soon.

5.2.2 *Example: Generalizing the badge rules*

We have too much duplication across the different badges. For example, QualityHero and SecurityCop are basically the same in terms of code and structure. We should generalize them. In both cases, the badge is assigned if the participant has taken a selected list of training courses. Therefore, our generalization needs a list of courses and the badge that should be assigned.

The BadgeForTrainings class does what we just described: it receives the list of training courses and the badge to give in its constructor. The give() method loops through the list of courses and checks whether they were all taken. Then badgeToGive() returns the badge provided through the constructor. To instantiate the concrete QualityHero badge rule, we need to instantiate BadgeForTrainings and provide it with the list of training courses this badge requires: in this case, testing and code quality.

Listing 5.7 `BadgeForTrainings` implementation

```
class BadgeForTrainings implements BadgeRule {
  private final List<String> trainings;
  private final Badge badgeToGive;
  public BadgeForTrainings(List<String> trainings,
   Badge badgeToGive) {                          ◁──  The constructor
    this.trainings = trainings;                        receives the list of
    this.badgeToGive = badgeToGive;                    trainings and badge.
  }
  public boolean give(Employee employee) {
    TrainingsTaken trainingsTaken = employee.getTrainingsTaken();
    return trainings.stream()
      .allMatch(training -> trainingsTaken.has(training));  ◁──  If all trainings
  }                                                               have been taken,
  public Badge badgeToGive() {                                    the method
    return badgeToGive;        ◁──  Returns the badge            returns true, or
  }                                that should be given          false otherwise.
}
var qualityHero = new BadgeForTrainings(
   Arrays.asList("TESTING", "CODE QUALITY"),
   Badge.QUALITY_HERO);              ◁───  Concrete QualityHero badge rule
var securityCop = new BadgeForTrainings(
   Arrays.asList("SECURITY 101", "SECURITY FOR MOBILE DEVS"),
   Badge.SECURITY_COP);         ◁──
                                    │  Concrete SecurityCop badge rule
```

We can apply the same strategy to the badges based on quantity and training. In the implementation of BadgeForQuantity in the next listing, the constructor receives the number of training courses the employee must have completed to get the badge, along with the badge. Then `give()` checks whether the employee has done so.

Listing 5.8   `BadgeForQuantity` **implementation**

```
class BadgeForQuantity implements BadgeRule {
  private final int quantity;
  private final Badge badgeToGive;
  public BadgeForQuantity(int quantity,
   Badge badgeToGive) {
    this.quantity = quantity;
    this.badgeToGive = badgeToGive;
  }
  public boolean give(Employee employee) {
    TrainingsTaken trainingsTaken = employee.getTrainingsTaken();
    return trainingsTaken.totalTrainings() >= quantity;
  }
  public Badge badgeToGive() {
    return badgeToGive;
  }
}
var fiveTrainings = new BadgeForQuantity(5, Badge.FIVE_TRAININGS);
```

The constructor receives the number of trainings required for this badge, and the badge.

Returns true if the number of trainings the employee has taken is greater than the provided quantity

We can instantiate concrete badges for quantity rules.

With the generalized badge rules, the next step is to assemble the final `BadgeGiver` with all the concrete rules. Before, when we had one class per rule and lots of duplication, instantiating them wasn't hard. If the system were using a dependency injection framework, all we would need to do would be to ask for all implementations of `BadgeRule`, and the framework would find them. However, with the generalized versions, we need smarter logic to instantiate the concrete rules and get the data from the database.

There are different ways to achieve that, ranging from simple and less flexible, with some human intervention, to more complex but more flexible and automated. One approach is to create a factory method: we can create factories for each type of badge rule, and these factories are responsible for instantiating them. (To learn more, see https://refactoring.guru/design-patterns/factory-method.)

The following listing shows the factories for `BadgeForTrainings` and `BadgeForQuantity`. `BadgeRuleFactory` describes what a factory should look like. Then, each concrete implementation–`BadgeForQuantityFactory` and `BadgeForTrainingsFactory`—gets its data from the database and returns a list with all the concrete rules.

Listing 5.9 `BadgeRuleFactory`

Factory interface

```
interface BadgeRuleFactory {
  List<BadgeRule> createRules();
}
class BadgeForQuantityFactory implements BadgeRuleFactory {
  public List<BadgeRule> createRules() {
    // accesses the DB, gets the data
    // and for each of them, instantiates a BadgeForQuantity class
    // ...
  }
}
class BadgeForTrainingsFactory implements BadgeRuleFactory {
  public List<BadgeRule> createRules() {
    // accesses the DB, gets the data
    // and for each of them, instantiates a BadgeForTrainings class
    // ...
  }
}
```

The BadgeForQuantityFactory instantiates all concrete badge rules based on quantity.

The BadgeForTrainingsFactory instantiates all concrete badge rules based on trainings.

Figure 5.3 illustrates the final class design of the badge rules. Note how easy it is to extend the system with more types of rules. All we have to do is create a new implementation of `BadgeRule` describing the high-level business rule for a badge and a `BadgeRuleFactory` that gets the current concrete rules for that badge.

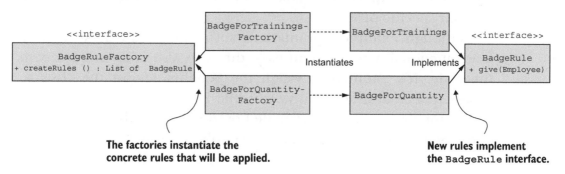

Figure 5.3 **The final class design of** `BadgeRule` **and** `BadgeRuleFactory`

With some creativity, we can even make a design force developers to create a factory whenever a new badge rule is created. This is one example of how to do it, but as I said before, it's okay to start with simple glue code and make it more sophisticated later if needed. We also haven't talked about infrastructure so far (that's the topic of chapter 6). Still, if your design doesn't allow factories to access the database, you can add one extra layer between the factory and the database access.

Good abstractions equal easier maintenance!

5.3   *Prefer simple abstractions*

> *Abstractions should be simple and require their implementations to do as little work as possible. Such abstractions simplify the creation of new concrete implementations and reduce the overall complexity of the code that may accumulate over time when the number of implementations grows.*

Abstractions add complexity to code. It's harder for developers to follow a flow full of interfaces and polymorphic calls. But this is the tradeoff you make in exchange for more flexibility. You should strive to simplify the abstraction as much as possible by letting it represent only the bare minimum of behavior and delegating the rest to concrete implementations.

5.3.1   *Rules of thumb*

Choosing the best design can be tricky and often involves tradeoffs. Ultimately, it's up to you to decide which tradeoffs are most suitable for your specific problem.

Although extension points and abstractions can make adding new functionality to a system easy, they can also add complexity to the code. It's essential to weigh the benefits against the costs to ensure that an abstraction is worthwhile.

It's not always easy to anticipate how much flexibility a system will need. Sometimes we implement a simplistic design that could use more flexibility or overcomplicate a design that doesn't need it.

To help you decide when to create extension points and abstractions, I suggest following the three rules of thumb illustrated in figure 5.4.

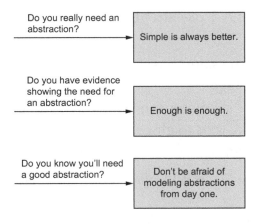

Figure 5.4   Three rules to help you decide whether to create an abstraction or extension point

5.3.2   Simple is always better

Keeping your code simple is always the best option. Don't create an abstraction without a clear reason to abstract the code. If you aren't sure how much flexibility you need, starting simple may be good enough.

But it's hard to define what *simple* means. Unfortunately, I often see code that lacks abstractions with an excuse of simplicity: for example, code full of if statements or long classes to avoid creating an interface. Sandi Metz, a Ruby developer who also authored books on object-oriented design, once said that duplication is cheaper than wrong abstraction (https://sandimetz.com/blog/2016/1/20/the-wrong-abstraction). Although this is true, remember that duplication is also more expensive than a good abstraction.

You shouldn't fall into this trap. Simple and small code isn't enough in places where an abstraction is needed.

5.3.3   Enough is enough

If you doubt whether an abstraction is needed, you can wait for empirical evidence. For example, when implementing the first discount rule for the e-book store, we don't need more than simple code. If we're then asked to implement a second discount rule, that's fine; maybe two are all we'll ever need. But when discount rules 3, 4, and 5 come in, and we start writing many if statements in a row, it may be time to rethink and go for an abstraction.

Here are some other things I pay attention to when deciding if it's time for an abstraction:

- Do I keep changing to the same class again and again?
- Do classes keep getting bigger?
- Am I constantly using `if` statements to implement variability?
- Do I keep finding clunky ways to glue existing business rules to other parts of the system?

This is far from an exhaustive list, but I hope it gives you a good idea of what to look out for.

Deciding when enough is enough is relative and a decision full of tradeoffs. If you make an early decision, there's a chance you are overengineering. If you take too long, it can require more effort for you to refactor the existing code.

5.3.4   *Don't be afraid of modeling abstractions from day one*

Sometimes you'll be confident from the start that you need flexibility. In these cases, don't be afraid of proposing an abstraction or extension point, even if you have only one or two implementations at the beginning.

If you opt to start with simple code, you may only delay the inevitable. Such a decision can cost you more than an immediately flexible solution.

5.3.5   *Example: Revisiting the badge example*

The design we created around badges in PeopleGrow! followed the ideas discussed in this chapter:

- The `BadgeRule` interface is straightforward. It's easy to create new implementations. The interface requires minimal information from clients (the employee under evaluation) and returns only what clients of the abstraction need (whether to give the badge, and the badge itself).
- The generalization of specific badge rules, such as the badge for trainings (implemented in the `BadgeForTrainings` class) and the badge for quantity (in `BadgeForQuantity`) are also simple in terms of implementation. They are decoupled from each other

and won't change if a new badge rule is created or because of a change in another badge rule.

- `BadgeGiver` can work with any badge rule and doesn't have to change if new badges are plugged in or unplugged.

The fun part of designing abstractions is that there are many ways to solve the same problem. If you were to do this yourself, your final design would likely be different from mine. Which is better, yours or mine? It's hard to say—we should always keep learning from our abstractions in the wild.

5.4 *Exercises*

Think through the following questions or discuss them with a colleague:

1. How often do you encounter well-designed extension points in your current software system? What do they look like?
2. Would parts of your current project deserve a better abstraction or extension point? What part? Why? How would you design it?
3. Have you ever suffered from a poorly designed abstraction? What did it look like? Why was it wrong?

Summary

- Abstractions and extension points simplify software evolution and prevent code complexity over time by allowing new functionality to be added without changing existing code.
- These design elements can be applied in various aspects of the system for flexibility, such as adding discount rules or generalizing specific rules for multiple instances.
- Simplicity should be a priority when designing abstractions and extension points, to avoid adding unnecessary complexity to the code.
- Introducing an abstraction early on can be beneficial because not having one when you need it can be costly.

Handling external dependencies and infrastructure

This chapter covers

- Decoupling infrastructure code from the domain
- Understanding how far to go when decoupling infrastructure
- Creating wrappers on top of infrastructure libraries and data structures

Software systems rarely exist in isolation; they often interact with databases for data persistence or web services from external companies or internal teams. A significant challenge in software design is preventing our code from being contaminated by these outside details.

You may wonder why this is a problem. There are a few reasons to protect your domain from external influences. First, they can impede your ability to replace a component with something simpler, which would facilitate testing. For instance, if you lack a layer between the code that accesses an external web service and your domain logic, it becomes difficult to test the domain logic in isolation.

Second, without encapsulation, your code becomes tightly coupled to the data structures and abstractions of third-party APIs. Many libraries are not particularly stable and undergo frequent changes. You don't want minor updates to those libraries affecting numerous places in your code.

Third, handling infrastructure involves low-level code, and without proper encapsulation, making changes becomes cumbersome. Consider a caching layer: you may start with a straightforward implementation using an in-memory hash map for quick access. However, as your application grows and requires more advanced caching strategies, you'd prefer to implement a new approach without needing to modify every instance where the old caching is used.

You may now think that all you need to do is add an interface to abstract the infrastructure, and you're done. Although this is a good starting point and often sufficient, I'd like to delve deeper into the topic.

A well-designed abstraction should hide the details of the infrastructure, allowing the rest of the system to remain largely unaware of it. However, there's an interesting tradeoff between proposing a simple interface that completely abstracts away the infrastructure (enabling easy evolution or even full replacement) and losing the ability to use specific features of the underlying infrastructure.

For example, you may want to take advantage of the performance of your Oracle database or the scalability of Amazon Simple Queue Service (SQS) queues. However, doing so may require a specific implementation that doesn't apply to any other database or queue. The challenge lies in creating abstractions that allow you to harness the benefits of the underlying infrastructure while avoiding contamination of your code with these specific details.

Furthermore, although I've used external systems (databases, caches, web services) as examples thus far, similar challenges can arise within your software system. Perhaps you're using an opinionated framework that imposes a coding style that isn't ideal for your domain code. Your design should shield you from such limitations as well.

Designing a solid infrastructure abstraction is akin to organizing the plumbing in your house. It involves ensuring organization, ease of maintenance, and replaceability. In this chapter, we explore how to create abstractions that will help make your code independent of specific external systems so your designs don't break when major changes happen in them.

> **Using "infrastructure" as a generic term**
>
> Throughout this chapter, I use terms like *infrastructure* and *infrastructure code*. By *infrastructure*, I mean any infrastructure or external system your software depends on, such as a database like Postgres, Redis as cache, or an external web service provided by an airline company that your software has to integrate with. By *infrastructure code*, I mean the code you write on your side to integrate with this external system. For example, you have to write database APIs and SQL queries so your application can read data from and write data into Postgres.

6.1   Separate infrastructure from the domain code

Code that handles infrastructure should be separated from the domain code. These classes should be as thin as possible and contain no business logic. This separation keeps the design clean, easier to evolve, and more testable.

Don't write any infrastructure-handling code inside any class with business logic. This is rule number one regarding handling infrastructure code—and a no-brainer because it's easy to follow and pays off quickly. Instead, write the handling code in a class whose sole purpose is to represent the communication between your application and the external system.

Even before we dive into a discussion of whether you need an interface or if the concrete class representing the external system is enough, you can improve your design by an order of magnitude just by putting the domain and infrastructure code in different classes. Your code is more testable because it's easier to replace a concrete class with a fake or a mock during testing, and any changes in the infrastructure code happen in a single place.

Separating infrastructure code from domain logic is common in more modern codebases. It's been years since I've seen a system that contains SQL queries and database logic code mixed with business rule code. Patterns like Data Access Objects and Repositories (from the book *Domain-Driven Design*) are prevalent in most codebases.

However, the devil is in the details. Let's say you need to retrieve a simple configuration value from a file to process business rules. It's common to see file-access logic and business logic mixed together. Although this may not appear to be a major problem, you've inadvertently coupled your code to the file's structure. This can complicate your life if the file needs to evolve because you'll have to locate all the places that read the file and make corresponding changes. Moreover, it becomes more challenging to test your code as you can't easily replace the configuration value to facilitate testing. To avoid these problems, you can introduce a `Configuration` class that encapsulates the logic of reading the configuration value from the file and returns it cleanly to the client.

Now, let's consider a scenario where you need to retrieve data using a third-party library provided by an external company. An inattentive developer may make direct method calls to this library within the business logic. Similar to the previous example, if the library changes, you'll have to update all the classes in your system accordingly. However, this problem could have been prevented if a single class handled all the calls to the library.

In a nutshell, aim to minimize the effect of these external systems on your code. By doing so, if these systems ever need to change, the resulting effect will be as minimal as possible.

6.1.1 *Do you need an interface?*

It's a good idea to have an interface that explicitly separates the infrastructure from the domain code. Although many argue that interfaces support us in changing the infrastructure's implementation later, the primary reason I use interfaces is that they prevent me from writing code that relies on the infrastructure directly. Within an interface, I can only define a set of methods I anticipate from the infrastructure, and nothing more.

Let's consider a scenario where we're tasked with implementing a feature that requires obtaining a list of employees. We know this list is stored in a database, so our code needs to interact with this external system. One approach to implementing this (depicted in figure 6.1) is to define an `EmployeeRepository` interface with a method `Set<Employee> allEmployees()`. Additionally, we have a concrete implementation—let's call it `HibernateEmployeeRepository`—which implements this interface and internally uses Hibernate to communicate with the database in the background. By using this interface, we ensure that no details related to the database leak into the domain code.

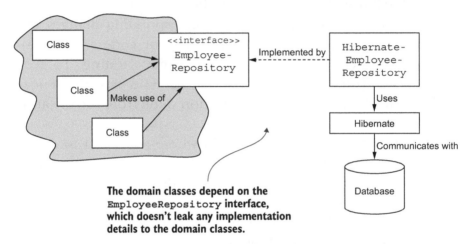

Figure 6.1 The `EmployeeRepository` **interface prevents implementation details from leaking into the domain.**

Different architectures, such as ports and adapters (also known as *hexagonal architecture*) and clean architecture, suggest the same idea: an interface that speaks the domain language and prevents implementation details from leaking.

That being said, always having an interface is not a hard rule you can't break. Sometimes a class is good enough. As long as this class speaks the domain language and doesn't allow implementation details to leak, you're fine.

My rules of thumb for when to create an interface are the following (also see figure 6.2):

- If I anticipate multiple implementations of the same infrastructure, I immediately implement an interface. Doing so ensures a smoother transition when additional implementations arise and also enables me to create a fake implementation of that infrastructure for testing purposes.
- If I have limited knowledge about the specific infrastructure details, the interface provides a solid starting point. It allows me to proceed with coding the rest of the features without being hindered by my lack of knowledge.
- When I know I'll use this infrastructure in multiple places, relying on an interface is more lightweight than relying on a heavy class that brings numerous dependencies.
- If the underlying infrastructure is complex, it becomes more challenging to prevent details from leaking. By employing an interface, I am compelled to carefully consider the design from day one.

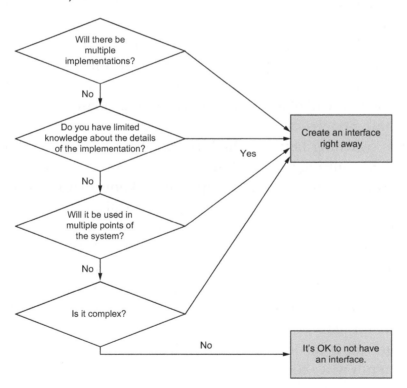

Figure 6.2 Deciding whether there's a need for an interface

With or without the interface, you must ensure that the code is well encapsulated and that the implementation details are hidden from the code but not from the developers.

6.1.2   *Hide details from the code, not from the developers*

Your design should conceal the internal details of the infrastructure from the rest of the code to minimize the effect of implementation changes. However, it's important not to hide too much from developers, because understanding what's happening behind the scenes enables them to write optimal and efficient code.

A common misconception in infrastructure-related code design is the belief that everything must be hidden from everyone. The primary objective of properly encapsulating infrastructure is to ensure that changes have a limited effect on the overall system. Your entire system shouldn't require extensive modifications when upgrading the version of your persistence framework, introducing read replicas to the database, or transitioning from SOAP to REST for a consumed web service.

But simultaneously, you don't want to hide everything from developers. Such an approach can be impractical and unnecessary for most projects. For instance, if developers know that a relational database is used instead of a document-oriented database, they may optimize their designs accordingly. Creating a design that supports seamless switching between different database types is possible but expensive, requiring a compelling business reason to implement.

Consider another example. Suppose we know that retrieving the list of employees involves making a remote call to the `Employee` service. In that case, we may exert additional effort to ensure that our code handles common failures in distributed architectures. We can create abstractions and components that make a remote call appear local to the rest of the system (although it may not always be achievable), but doing so correctly demands significant effort that isn't necessary for most systems. Moreover, if developers are unaware that a remote call is involved in retrieving the employee list, they may inadvertently write code that doesn't function correctly from the start.

The extent to which to abstract infrastructure is a topic of heated debate within the community. On the one hand, some advocate treating infrastructure as a mere detail not warranting excessive concern while modeling the rest of the system. On the other hand, some proponents assert that infrastructure is an integral part of an information system that should be accepted as such.

My viewpoint lies somewhere in between these perspectives. I agree that infrastructure should not be treated as a mere detail. For example, databases are core components of information systems. However, we also don't want the implementation details scattered throughout the codebase. Instead, we should isolate infrastructure-specific code as much as possible to minimize the effect of changes, similar to what we discussed in the previous section.

6.1.3 Changing the infrastructure someday: Myth or reality?

The strong encapsulation of the infrastructure code is beneficial when changes become necessary. In such cases, the goal is to modify only the classes related to the infrastructure while ensuring that the rest of the system continues to function seamlessly.

But complete infrastructure overhauls are rare, so why optimize for such scenarios? This is a valid point. Most software systems seldom undergo complex migrations, such as transitioning from one type of database to another or switching web frameworks. Nevertheless, the infrastructure of most software systems undergoes constant evolution over time.

> **Testing and infrastructure**
>
> From a testing perspective, your infrastructure is constantly changing. For example, you may not want your unit tests to depend on a Kafka instance.

I can think of many evolutions in infrastructure that we want to implement without breaking the rest of the system, including the following examples:

- The system requires caching, and we wish to cache specific queries without altering the entire codebase.

- Scaling demands necessitate the introduction of a read replica. We don't want to change every place in the code that calls the database and redirects it to the replica. Instead, we want the infrastructure abstraction to handle it.
- The authentication mechanism used internally by our company to validate calls from internal web services has changed. It shouldn't be necessary to modify every occurrence of a call due to this change.
- The system now needs to handle large file uploads and downloads, prompting a decision to transition to Amazon's S3 instead of storing files on on-premises disks. This migration becomes much easier if the infrastructure code is encapsulated behind a well-defined interface.

Even if you're sure your infrastructure won't change drastically, remember that it will evolve, and you want to minimize the evolution cost.

6.1.4   *Example: Database access and the message bot*

From the start, we kept infrastructure code separate in all the code examples in PeopleGrow! We didn't want those implementation details to clutter the entire codebase. This applies not just to infrastructure code but also to everything we've talked about in this chapter. Let's review.

From a domain point of view, the repository interfaces represent all the required data access behavior. For example, the `EmployeeRepository` interface in listing 6.1 has methods such as `findById`, which returns the employee with that ID, `findByLastName`, which returns all employees with a specific last name, and `save`, which persists a new employee to the database.

Note that this interface doesn't give any hints about how these methods are implemented. Which database is behind them? Which library is used to communicate with them? If we ever need to change any implementation detail related to accessing employee information in the database, the rest of the system won't be affected by the changes.

Listing 6.1   The `EmployeeRepository` interface

```
interface EmployeeRepository {                        ◄─┐   This interface models all the
    Employee findById(int id);                          │   data access actions related
    Set<Employee> findByLastName(String lastName);      │   to employees.
    void save(Employee employee);
    // ...
}
```

PeopleGrow! is definitely in a good position if we need to change how we handle database access. Behind the scenes, PeopleGrow! uses Hibernate as a persistence framework and Postgres as its database of choice. `HibernateEmployeeRepository` contains all the handling code.

Suppose we now want to improve the performance of the `findBy-LastName` method, and we decide to add some caching. All we need to do is change the implementation of this method, hitting a cache first and, if it's not there, hitting the database. We plug our caching library into the `Cache` class.

Listing 6.2   Changing some infrastructure details

HibernateEmployeeRepository now
depends on our Cache library.

```
class HibernateEmployeeRepository implements EmployeeRepository {
    private Cache cache;                               ◄─┘
    // ...
    public Set<Employee> findByLastName(String lastName) {   ◄─┐   We go for the
        if (!cache.contains(lastName)) {                       │   cache first
            cache.add(lastName, session                        │   and then the
                .createQuery("from Employee e where e.lastName = ...")   │   database.
                .setParameter(...)
                .toSet());
        }
        return cache.get(lastName);
    }
}
```

Thanks to this separation between infrastructure and domain code, we only needed to modify `HibernateEmployeeRepository`; the rest of the codebase remained untouched.

I won't get into the details of how to implement caching or what challenges it brings to the implementation because this isn't the focus of this book. Introducing caching in a real system may be more complex than in this example. Nevertheless, changing code in a single place rather than everywhere is already a great advantage, as shown in figure 6.3.

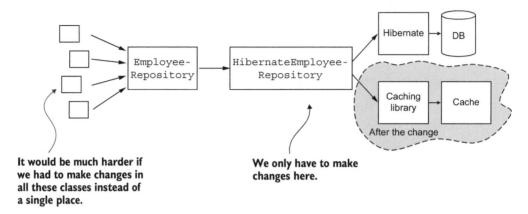

It would be much harder if we had to make changes in all these classes instead of a single place.

We only have to make changes here.

Figure 6.3   Changes only have to happen in a single place, not the entire system.

A challenge that emerges when modeling an interface to hide the details is that we may design an interface that doesn't use the infrastructure to its fullest. And we don't want that.

6.2   *Use the infrastructure fully*

Get to know your underlying infrastructure and use it to the best advantage. Design your classes in a way that optimizes what they have to offer. This helps you to write the best system you can with the least effort.

Most software systems rely on existing components to fulfill their tasks. For instance, they depend on databases for data persistence and web frameworks to efficiently build APIs. These components have undergone significant advancements in recent decades, providing developers with a wealth of features that would be a shame to disregard simply because they don't fit our class design.

Let's consider a scenario where we need to perform a data operation, and our database offers a remarkable feature that can help us do so correctly and efficiently. The alternative approach would be to load the data into the system and perform the operation purely through code, thus avoiding polluting our design with a feature specific to that particular database. Although this may make the design appear clean and technology independent, it will ultimately complicate our work and degrade the quality of the system. The second option is significantly slower and more susceptible to bugs than the first. Unless there's a valid reason to do so, you shouldn't overlook the advantages the infrastructure offers. The challenge lies in using your infrastructure to its fullest potential without compromising the integrity of your design.

6.2.1 *Do your best not to break your design*

In the world of software design, nothing comes without tradeoffs. If you wish to use a remarkable feature from your infrastructure, it may require creating additional abstractions. This ensures that your design remains protected if there are changes in how this operation is handled in the future, which is not uncommon.

Technically speaking, an interface that provides a domain-focused operation implemented by a class encapsulating the handling code is often sufficient. For instance, let's consider a scenario where we need to generate a report that aggregates information from multiple tables, and our database offers a perfect solution. Similar to the approach taken with the employee list, one design idea is to create an interface called `ReportGenerator` with a domain-focused method like `Report generateReport()`. A concrete class implements this interface and uses the magical query capabilities of our database. If we need to change this in the future, such as by migrating to a database with fewer capabilities, we can create a new implementation of the interface to achieve the same outcome.

Notice how similar this is to the previous example of `Employee-Repository`. By creating domain-focused interfaces that emphasize the expected business outcomes and abstract away implementation details, many challenges related to using specific infrastructure features can be mitigated.

In information systems, a common challenge arises when we consider bypassing the aggregate and performing an operation directly on an aggregated object. For instance, using a direct database update command may be more performant than making a change through the aggregate root. However, I recommend revisiting your design before proceeding with such an approach.

Ask yourself whether the object needs to be part of the aggregate in the first place if you feel the change should be made directly within the object. This is often the appropriate response to this design challenge. Alternatively, you can consider eliminating the invariant. Not all invariants we initially consider are truly necessary. If the object must be part of the aggregate due to essential invariants, can you accept some eventual inconsistency and remodel it using domain events? Breaking your design should be a last resort and avoided at all costs.

6.2.2 Example: Cancelling an enrollment

As you may remember, PeopleGrow! lets employees cancel their enrollment in a training course. In chapter 3, we implemented a `cancel()` method in the `Offering` aggregate root to receive the employee who wants to skip the training, find them in the list of enrollments, remove them from the list, and add one available spot to the offering. This code is reproduced in the following listing.

> Listing 6.3 The cancel method in the `Offering` entity

```
class Offering {
  private List<Enrollment> enrollments;
  private int availableSpots;                      Removes the enrollment of an
  // ...                                            employee from the specific offering
  public void cancel(Employee employee) {    ◁───┘
    Enrollment enrollmentToCancel = findEnrollmentOf(employee);
    if(enrollmentToCancel == null)
      throw new EmployeeNotEnrolledException();
    Calendar now = Calendar.getInstance();                 Goes through all
    enrollmentToCancel.cancel(now);                        enrollments in the
    availableSpots++;                                      offering, looking
  }                                                        for the one for the
  private Enrollment findEnrollmentOf(Employee employee) {  ◁── employee
    // loops through the list of enrollments and
    // finds the one for that employee
    // ...
  }
}
```

We discussed in chapter 3 that this `cancel()` method isn't the most performant. After all, it needs to loop through the entire list of enrollments. There's a relational database behind the scenes, so we may need an extra query to bring this list into memory. We implemented this code because we considered the performance hit not to be a problem for such a small system. But PeopleGrow! is growing, and we can't afford that anymore.

The first idea that comes to the developers' minds is to move the entire canceling logic to a service class. The service will coordinate canceling the enrollment and then bump the number of available spots.

Listing 6.4   The cancel operation as a service

```
class CancelEnrollmentService {
  private OfferingRepository offerings;
  public void cancel(int offeringId, int employeeId) {      ◄──── The overall logic is similar to the previous cancel() method.
    if(offeringId==null || employeeId==null)
      throw new InvalidArgumentException();
    Offering offering = offerings.getById(offeringId);
    Enrollment enrollment =
      offerings.getEnrollment(offeringId, employeeId);      ◄──── Gets the enrollment directly from the database without having to load the entire list first
    if(enrollment == null)
      throw new EnrollmentDoesntExistException();
    enrollment.cancel(now());
    offering.increaseAvailableSpots();      ◄──── Bumps the number of available spots
  }
}
class Offering {
  // ...
  public void increaseAvailableSpots() {
    availableSpots++;
  }
}
```

Although this implementation no longer requires loading the complete list of enrollments, it does have some drawbacks. The most significant is that it reduces the control of invariants in the aggregate root. With this implementation, any client can now manipulate the available spots by requesting an increase. Additionally, this approach may introduce inconsistencies. For instance, what happens if we load the list of enrollments in another part of the business logic and then the cancellation service is invoked? The list of enrollments in the offering may become outdated because we don't reload it when removing an offering from the service. Finally, the implementation of getEnrollment had to be included in OfferingRepository because we typically don't have repositories for internal parts of the aggregate. We usually handle them through the aggregate root, which isn't ideal.

Transferring the control of invariants out of the aggregate root may seem like the easiest solution, but it can quickly result in inconsistent objects. As discussed in chapter 3, we must do our best to avoid this. However, I understand why it happens. Refactoring a settled design can be challenging. Nonetheless, investing in refactoring and eliminating any possibilities of object inconsistencies will pay off, even in the short term. The payoff will depend on how important or frequently used the aggregate is within the entire system.

Let's try to redesign the code. The problem seems to originate from the need to keep the list of free spots up to date in the Offering entity. Do we really need this information in the entity? If we take available-Spots out of the entity, the problem becomes simpler. We can then promote enrollments to an aggregate. Whenever a request to cancel an enrollment comes in, an application service can grab the offering and the enrollment and cancel it. The next listing is the implementation of CancelEnrollmentService.

Listing 6.5   `CancelEnrollmentService` application service

```
class CancelEnrollmentService {
  private OfferingRepository offerings;
  private EnrollmentRepository enrollments;
  public void cancel(int offeringId, int employeeId) {     ⟵  The cancel() method
    if(offeringId==null || employeeId==null)                    organizes the workflow.
      throw new InvalidArgumentException();
    Offering offering = offerings.getById(offeringId);
    if(offering == null)
        throw new OfferingDoesntExistException();
    Enrollment enrollment =
      offerings.getEnrollment(offeringId, employeeId);
    if(enrollment == null)
        throw new EnrollmentDoesntExistException();        ⟵  We cancel the enrollment
    Calendar now = Calendar.getInstance();                     directly as it's now its own
    enrollment.cancel(now);                            ⟵      aggregate.
  }
}
class Offering {                          ⟵  The Offering class no longer has
  // private int availableSpots;              the availableSpots attribute and
  // public void cancel(Enrollment enrollmentToCancel) { ... }  the cancel method.
}
```

The number of available spots can easily be calculated by a SQL query in the Postgres database behind the scenes. We then create an availableSpots(Offering) method in OfferingRepository. In the

concrete `HibernateOfferingRepository` implementation of that repository, we'll use Hibernate's query language to get that information.
Internally, the class even caches the results to speed up the response.

Listing 6.6 Calculating the available spots via SQL query

```
class HibernateOfferingRepository implements OfferingRepository {
  private Session session;
  public int availableSpots(Offering offering) {
    if(!cache.contains(offering)) {
      int spots = (int) session
        .createQuery("select maximumNumberOfAttendees - " +
          "count(...) from Offering o where ...")
        .setParameter(...)
        .getSingleResult();
      cache.put(offering, spots);
    }
    return cache.get(offering);
  }
}
```

Uses Hibernate's HQL to query the database and get the number of available spots

Caches the result to improve performance

There are other ways to model this. For example, we could keep the
`availableSpots` attribute in the `Offering` entity and use domain events
to update both aggregates. Once a cancel request came in, the
domain service would publish a domain event, and different listen-
ers would update the offering and the enrollment. That might mean
eventually consistent information, but users might be fine with it.

> **Defining errors out of existence**
>
> In chapter 3, we explored the idea of defining errors out of existence.
> We can apply that idea here. The `cancel()` method currently throws an
> exception if the offering or employee is null. This means clients should
> handle this possible exception. Another way of designing this method
> would be to make it do nothing if an inexistent offering or employee
> was passed, simplifying the clients' lives.

As always, there are no rights and wrongs, only tradeoffs.

6.3 Only depend on things you own

Create wrappers on top of third-party data structures and libraries.
Doing so prevents third-party dependencies from spreading too far in the
codebase, saving you time whenever such out-of-control classes change.

Our systems benefit greatly from the availability of third-party libraries and systems. Many libraries even provide software development kits (SDKs) that simplify the integration process. However, it's important to remember that these libraries also bring code that is outside your control. You have no influence over the library's release cycle or the possibility of introducing breaking changes.

Therefore, when incorporating code from other libraries and systems, it's crucial to establish a layer that prevents their proliferation throughout your codebase. These wrappers ensure that any changes in the library code will only affect this specific layer and nothing else.

Let's consider an example where we are integrating with a payment gateway that offers a clean library to streamline the integration process. To initiate a payment, this library requires us to invoke the `makePayment()` method and provide a `PaymentDetails` data structure containing information such as the payment amount, currency, buyer's email, and other relevant details. However, we don't want the `Payment-Details` class, which we don't own, to be scattered throughout the codebase. In this case, we need to create a class that encompasses the same information and pass it to our `PaymentGateway` class (an *adapter*) to convert the information into the appropriate API calls expected by the library. See figure 6.4.

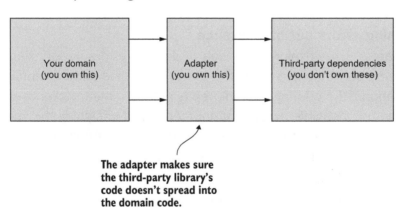

The adapter makes sure the third-party library's code doesn't spread into the domain code.

Figure 6.4   The adapter prevents the library code from getting spread into the domain.

At first, these wrappers may appear redundant. After all, our data structure resembles the one used by the library. However, it's important to recognize that we have complete control over our data structure and can manage its changes. If the library undergoes modifications, such as requiring an additional function call, we only need to update the adapter.

Certain changes in the library may necessitate modifications in other areas of the application. For instance, let's say the payment gateway now requires an extra piece of information. In such a case, we must incorporate this information into our data structure and find the appropriate location in our code to load it. Nevertheless, these changes are significantly more within our control.

Additionally, libraries often become deprecated or undergo complete rewrites. If such a situation occurs, it is much easier to make the necessary adjustments in the adapter rather than locating and modifying all the different parts of the application that use the library.

6.3.1 *Don't fight your frameworks*

Although it's important to minimize coupling to external dependencies you don't control, it's equally essential to avoid fighting against them. Complete decoupling from all dependencies is an unattainable goal.

Attempting to achieve full decoupling can significantly increase the complexity of your code by orders of magnitude. Moreover, your abstractions may fall short of meeting your requirements at some point.

As a developer, it is necessary to balance accepting dependencies you acknowledge will exist and challenging dependencies you are unwilling to accept. Let me illustrate how I approach this with a few examples:

- If I have chosen Spring MVC as my model-view-controller (MVC) framework, I don't attempt excessive decoupling from it. I use all the capabilities that Spring provides to their fullest extent. Although I avoid using Spring code in my domain objects (such as entities and services), I don't shy away from using Spring's helpful utilities in my controllers.
- If I have selected Hibernate as my persistence framework and Postgres as my database, I encapsulate Hibernate code within the repository or data access object classes to isolate it from the rest of the system. However, I don't ignore the fact that there's

an object-relational mapping mechanism at work or that I have a robust relational database supporting my system.

- If I need to integrate with a third-party payment gateway using its provided library, which may be less stable than large-scale open source frameworks and subject to frequent changes (due to the ever-evolving nature of payment systems), I add a wrapper layer on top of it and ensure that no other parts of the code directly depend on it.

- If the system requires generating reports in Excel files, I design domain-specific data structures to represent the report information and encapsulate the Excel generation code within an adapter. I don't expose the specific library for generating the file to the rest of the codebase.

- If I have opted for Amazon AWS as my cloud provider, I don't disregard its powerful capabilities. I fully use Amazon SQS (AWS's queue) and make architectural decisions that favor SQS. However, I encapsulate the relevant code within an adapter to prevent AWS-specific code from spreading throughout the codebase.

Note that these are personal approaches and not absolute truths. You may have different arguments and make different decisions in the given scenarios. Nonetheless, the general principle applies: minimize dependencies on external components you don't own, and work harmoniously with your chosen frameworks and architectural decisions.

6.3.2 Be aware of indirect leakage

Interfaces can effectively prevent the rest of the code from knowing about or depending on implementation details, but these details can still leak into the code. Let's consider the example of object-relational mapping (ORM) frameworks. ORMs often perform tasks behind the scenes that developers may not be aware of and that can affect the rest of their code. For instance, when we return a Hibernate-managed entity to the rest of our code, even if our code isn't aware that the entity is managed by Hibernate, it remains connected to Hibernate's session and may be automatically persisted when the transaction scope is closed. Another common scenario is client code invoking a getter method in a Hibernate-managed entity and triggering the framework to execute additional queries to the database without the developer's explicit knowledge. We may not see these behaviors from the code itself, but the underlying infrastructure's behavior indirectly seeps into our code.

It's up to you to determine whether this is favorable or undesirable and to what extent you should safeguard your design against it. In the example mentioned, if you find this kind of leakage undesirable, you can introduce an additional layer to ensure that Hibernate never manages entities used within the domain code. This requirement would be part of the contract defined by the interface, which the concrete class implementing it and using Hibernate internally must adhere to. Although it requires extra effort, it provides an added level of flexibility. If you ever decide to transition from Hibernate to another framework, your domain code will remain unaffected.

As mentioned, these implementation details should be hidden from the code but never from the developer. Once again, developers must have a thorough understanding of their infrastructure choices and their implications for the overall design.

6.3.3   *Example: Message bot*

If you recall PeopleGrow!'s message bot implementation, you may have noticed that we made sure the data structures of the Bot SDK didn't spread across the codebase. The ChatBotV1 class provided by the SDK requires a BotMessage class to write a message via the bot. ChatBotV1 and BotMessage are third-party classes we have little control over, so we did what's best. The Bot interface doesn't let them leak into the domain. They are well encapsulated into the SDKBot concrete implementation. The following listing shows the code.

Listing 6.7   SDKBot implementation

```
interface Bot {
  void sendPrivateMessage(String userId, String msg);
}
class SDKBot implements Bot {
  public void sendPrivateMessage(String userId, String msg) {
    var chatBot = new ChatBotV1();
    var message = new BotMessage(userId, msg);
    chatBot.writeMessage(message);
  }
}
```

Instantiate the chatbot class from the SDK

Composes the BotMessage, also part of the SDK

Sends it to the bot via the SDK's provided writeMessage() method

Although this may look like code duplication because `sendPrivate-Method` requires the precise information that the `BotMessage` data structure needs, you never know what tomorrow will look like. If a change is made in these third-party classes, we know the only place we'll need to change, and we will be better able to trace any other change required in the domain code if the `Bot` interface is also forced to change.

6.4   Encapsulate low-level infrastructure errors into high-level domain errors

> *Any errors triggered by the infrastructure must be fully encapsulated into the infrastructure layer, converted to an error that makes sense to the domain, and gracefully handled by the application.*

Infrastructures and the libraries that help us communicate with them (for example, a Postgres database, a JDBC driver that's used to communicate with it in Java, and Hibernate, a popular object-relational mapping framework that many teams use) may throw all sorts of errors and exceptions. This means the low-level infrastructure implementation must know about such errors. For example, if a database throws a unique-constraint exception whenever the constraint is violated, the infrastructure layer must be aware of and catch it.

Some errors may be recoverable, and we can take action directly in the infrastructure layer without popping the error up to higher layers. For example, if the database layer notices that the European cluster isn't available for a query, the layer can switch to the American cluster and execute the query there. Of course, we have to decide whether switching between clusters is desirable; but if so, encapsulating it in the infrastructure layer saves the rest of the code from knowing how this happens and allows this behavior to change more easily in the future.

Other types of errors are unrecoverable, and the best we can do is show an error message to the user and internally log the low-level details to facilitate debugging. In these cases, the infrastructure may throw a domain-focused exception containing helpful information to be displayed to the user while also logging relevant details to the developer.

Never let exception classes from your framework spread through your codebase. You don't want a `JdbcPostgresUniqueConstraint-Exception` or similar handled in upper layers. This prevents your code from being coupled to infrastructure decisions and your current framework. If you need to bubble up the constraint exception, the best alternative is to create a domain-focused exception—for example, `EmployeeAlreadyExistsException`, which is free of any infrastructure details.

6.4.1   *Example: Handling exceptions in SDKBot*

The `writeMessage` method of the `ChatBotV1` API may throw an `IOException`. Although this is a native Java exception, we don't want to let it spread. Let's handle it properly in the infrastructure code. If the exception happens, the code throws a `BotException` containing the user ID and the message that wasn't delivered and logs the low-level details of the original exception to the developer.

Listing 6.8   Revised `SDKBot` implementation

```
interface Bot {
  void sendPrivateMessage(String userId, String msg);
}
class SDKBot implements Bot {
  public void sendPrivateMessage(String userId, String msg) {
    try {
      var chatBot = new ChatBotV1();
      var message = new BotMessage(userId, msg);      Throws a domain-focused
      chatBot.writeMessage(message);                  exception and logs the
    } catch (IOException e) {            ◁────────────  low-level details
      throw new BotException(userId, message);
      LOGGER.error(e);
    }
  }
}                                                      BotException is a domain-
class BotException extends RuntimeException {  ◁─────  focused exception.
    ...
}
```

The implementation now prevents infrastructure errors from bubbling up to other layers.

6.5   *Exercises*

Think through the following questions or discuss them with a colleague:

1 Does your current project separate infrastructure from domain code? If not, what should you do to get there?

2 How far do you think developers should go when isolating infrastructure code? Can you make compromises? What are the tradeoffs involved?

3 What do you think of always encapsulating things you don't own? Is this a good idea or not? Why?

Summary

- Decouple any infrastructure-handling code from the domain code. Doing so reduces the effect of changes in the infrastructure code on the entire codebase.

- The infrastructure layer should hide the implementation details from other parts of the codebase. Developers should know what's behind the scenes, as understanding helps them develop better software systems.

- Don't let third-party libraries and data structures of external systems spread throughout your codebase. Create (domain-focused) wrappers around them.

- Don't fight your frameworks. You won't ever be able to decouple your system entirely. Instead, decide which tools and technologies you accept being coupled to and which you don't.

Achieving modularization

7

This chapter covers

- Designing modules that provide complex features through simple interfaces
- Reducing the dependencies between modules
- Defining ownership and engagement rules

Up to this point in our journey through simple object-oriented design, our discussions have primarily focused on simplicity, consistency, abstractions, and extension points. We discussed how to apply these ideas from small methods to a set of classes. However, as we venture into large, multifaceted systems, our scope must broaden. We must consider not just classes within a single component but also how different components that perform entirely different business operations interact and integrate.

Think of a large-scale business system that takes care of an e-commerce shop. The billing system, which handles charging customers, is complex and most likely developed by one dedicated

135

team. The same is true for the delivery system, which ensures that goods get to their buyers, and for the inventory system, which controls whether items are still available or if the shop has to restock them. Although these systems are different from each other, they must collaborate. The delivery system must consult with the inventory system before delivering goods. Billing must notify delivery that the invoice was paid and the goods can be delivered.

Picture each component as an individual player on a football team; each has a role to play, but their effectiveness is defined by how they coordinate and work together toward a common goal. As football players must understand their positions, responsibilities, and tactics, software components must also have well-defined roles. They need clear contracts about how to interact with others and what others can expect from them. This delineation helps components work harmoniously, ensuring that they collaborate without clashing. Importantly, it also allows for components to evolve and improve independently of one another. With a clear contract, a single component can be altered or upgraded without triggering a domino effect of changes across the entire system.

Neglecting the design of modules can lead to considerable difficulties down the line. Components that aren't designed with adequate care tend to become overly dependent on each other, leading to tight coupling. Changing a single module can be a Herculean task in a tightly coupled system because it may require changes in many other interconnected modules. This setup is also a breeding ground for bugs because developers are forced to understand the intricate workings of multiple modules before they can make even minor maintenance tweaks.

Remember that the principles we've discussed so far—simplicity, keeping things consistent, good abstractions and extension points, and isolating infrastructure details—are equally applicable at the module level. As we encapsulate data within a class, we can encapsulate related functionality within a module.

The design of individual components is undoubtedly essential. But in a large system, their collaboration brings about true harmony, just like in an orchestra. In this chapter, we repurpose the ideas discussed in earlier chapters so they make even more sense at the module level.

NOTE   In this chapter, the illustrative example comes at the end but uses all the principles introduced here.

7.1 *Build deep modules*

Modules should provide simple interfaces on top of complex features. The simple interface makes integrating other modules easier, reduces coupling, and simplifies their evolution. Modules should also be cohesive and own everything related to the functionality they expose.

A great module hides all the details of complex features and offers a simple interface that removes all the complexity from clients. Note that, at this level, I'm not talking about encapsulating complex business rules in a class. The concept is much bigger than that. I mean hiding an entire business behind a module. Continuing the example from the chapter introduction, in an e-commerce system, all the rules related to delivery should be in a Delivery module, and all the rules related to invoicing and payment should be in a Billing module.

Delivery and Billing are complex modules. If they have to collaborate, Delivery shouldn't need to deeply understand Billing and vice versa. The more straightforward an interface one module can provide to the other, the better it is for clients and for itself. It's easier for clients to integrate with the new module. And the simpler and leaner the interface is, the easier it is for developers to make changes without breaking all of its consumers.

Figure 7.1 illustrates what I mean by *deep modules.* Note the module's size and depth: it offers many complex features. But also note how thin and simple its API layer is: other modules only need to understand the API layer and nothing more.

The following subsections discuss the primary challenges of building deep modules: identifying what should be in the module, keeping related things close, designing clear and simple interfaces, keeping compatibility, and providing flexible ways to extend the module.

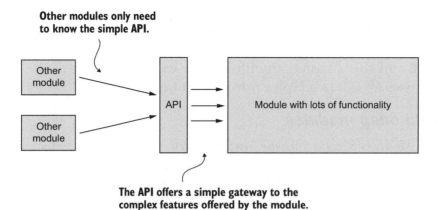

Other modules only need to know the simple API.

Other module

Other module

API

Module with lots of functionality

The API offers a simple gateway to the complex features offered by the module.

Figure 7.1   Modules should offer a simple API on top of complex features.

Deep modules

The term *deep module* comes from John Ousterhout's book *A Philosophy of Software Design*. John says that good modules are always "deep." A deep module provides powerful functionality under a simple interface. A shallow module, on the other hand, provides an interface that's almost as complex as the functionality it encapsulates. You don't want shallow modules because they increase the system's overall complexity without much benefit.

7.1.1   *Find ways to reduce the effects of changes*

Deciding what should be included in a module is as challenging as determining what should be in a class or method. Ideally, we want to minimize the number of modules that must be modified when a business domain changes. For example, if a new business rule emerges for invoices, we should only need to change the Invoice module; there should be no need to modify the Delivery module.

This often entails having modules that encompass entire business domains. All classes related to invoices should be in the same module, and all classes related to delivery should be in a dedicated Delivery module.

7.1.2 *Keep refining your domain boundaries*

It's undoubtedly hard to define a clear boundary between different business domains. Billing, Delivery, and Invoice may look completely different from each other in the simple example of this book, but in real life, domains are often strongly intertwined. I recommend working in strong collaboration with domain experts (they understand the business) and technical leads (they understand the pains that teams are having when trying to deliver working software), and keep revisiting your interpretation of the domain. An excellent reference on strategies to identify domain boundaries is the canonical book *Domain-Driven Design* by Eric Evans, in particular, sections 1 (putting the domain model to work) and 4 (strategic design).

7.1.3 *Keep related things close*

Another way to approach this principle is to ensure that related things or components that require simultaneous changes are kept close together. When we know that altering A necessitates modifying B, the change becomes easier and more predictable if A and B are nearby, such as in the same module.

There are advantages to keeping related things together. First, when A and B are in the same module, they are likely part of the same continuous integration, build process, and test pipelines. If a breaking change occurs or one class is modified without considering the other, a robust test suite will detect the problem. Conversely, if A and B are in different modules, these modules can be developed independently. Although there are methods to ensure that compilation or tests will fail if one class is changed but not the other, this approach is less straightforward.

Second, when A and B are in the same module, the module's developers probably have a comprehensive understanding of both classes. They know what needs to change and how to do it efficiently. Conversely, suppose A and B are separated and handled by different teams. In that case, no developer may have a complete picture in their mind, so they have to request changes from the other team or make them themselves with less confidence.

7.1.4   *Fight accidental coupling, or document it when you can't*

Although keeping related things in the same module seems straight-forward in theory, it is more nuanced in practice. Business domains are highly interconnected, and developers often need to couple different modules.

For example, suppose we need to ensure that changes made to the details of an invoice (such as adding a new attribute to represent the buyer's preferred address format) also reflect in the PDF generated by the Delivery module. We can contemplate various design alternatives to avoid this coupling, and that's great! The longer we can avoid coupling, the better. However, the reality is that you won't always be able to come up with optimal alternatives, especially considering budget constraints when developing a feature.

We will discuss technical approaches to ensure that changes in Invoice don't break the Delivery module, even if one is implemented before the other: for instance, designing backward and forward compatibility in how modules communicate. In addition, you must document such couplings the best you can. Add code comments in the codebase, create documentation in the team's wiki, and automate processes in your pipeline that alert you whenever you make a breaking change. Use whatever methods work best for you and your team.

7.2   *Design clear interfaces*

> *Modules should offer public interfaces that are easy to use, require as little information as possible from clients, and are stable. That simplifies the integration between two modules and reduces the chances of breaking changes.*

In large-scale software systems, modules need to communicate with each other to deliver the entire business workflow. Ensuring that a module effectively encapsulates entire business domains and that any changes to that domain only require modifications within the module is just part of the challenge. Another significant aspect is offering clear communication interfaces that enable modules to interact.

This interface is nothing more than the API a module provides to the external world. Implementation-wise, it can vary from simple classes and methods that a module offers other modules, to web APIs that support different request and response formats.

> ## APIs and monolithic systems
> Although the term *API* is commonly associated with remote HTTP calls, an API does not always have to be offered exclusively through a web API. In modular monolithic systems, good, old-fashioned method calls are used to exchange messages between modules.

A good communication interface has several key characteristics. First and foremost, it is simple. Clients don't need an in-depth understanding of how the module works, as the interface is designed to be easily understandable by anyone. This also avoids the need for complex input objects; if necessary, the API provides clean mechanisms to handle them.

In addition, a good communication interface maintains its initial promises and ensures good backward compatibility. It recognizes that clients will not change their code every time a module changes. Furthermore, it avoids breaking clients without ample prior warning.

Exemplary communication interfaces offer clear extension mechanisms. They allow clients to implement specific variations in the module's behavior without inconveniencing another module's development team or bloating the module with code that serves only a single client. We discuss these characteristics in more detail in the following sections.

7.2.1 Keep the module's interface simple

Keep the module's interface to the external world as simple as possible. The challenge in designing such interfaces is that modules encapsulate complex business logic by their very nature. Ensuring that the complexity does not leak outside the module is crucial.

Let's delve into what constitutes a simple interface for a module. The interface should not require knowledge of how the module operates internally. For example, suppose the Delivery module offers an API that provides information about whether the customer's goods were delivered. In that case, clients of this API should not be concerned with the underlying mechanisms for retrieving this information. Whether it comes from a database, another module's call, or cache utilization (for faster responses) should be inconsequential to clients.

A good interface is also easy to use. Clients should not be burdened with performing complex setups or invoking a convoluted chain of methods in a specific order for the module to fulfill its purpose. All the complexity should be handled within the module, minimizing the client's responsibilities. Suppose we need to expose a module feature that requires an intricate setup. In that case, it is important to ensure that most of the complexity resides within the module rather than encumbering the client.

When designing interfaces, remember that as soon as they are made public, other modules will begin to depend on them. Therefore, a good interface is stable: it undergoes minimal changes and does not force clients to continually update how they interact with the module. A good interface also offers backward compatibility.

7.2.2   *Backward-compatible modules*

Modularization offers numerous advantages. For example, it allows different teams to work on different parts of a product without interfering with one another excessively. However, it also presents the challenge of different parts of the system potentially residing in various locations—even in different codebases and repositories.

In a system with a single module, it is easier to identify all the places that need to be modified when a method changes. The compiler may signal an error because the method now expects three parameters instead of two. But determining when an API has changed in systems with multiple modules is more complex. Questions like "Who is using this API?" are harder to answer. Furthermore, in a single module, if we modify a method's contract, we naturally feel compelled to update all the places where it is called; otherwise, our code won't compile. Backward compatibility doesn't require constant consideration because we can modify the contract and update all its clients. We have full control over the entire process.

In larger modularized systems, however, we may not want or have the authority to modify other modules. We have to ask the team responsible for maintaining those modules, and this process can take weeks. Waiting for all the teams to update to the new API before we can deploy a new feature is not ideal.

Backward compatibility plays a vital role in large modularized systems. The API of a module should be able to understand requests compatible with its previous versions. This is crucial for scalable development. We don't want to wait for other teams to complete their tasks, and other teams don't want their systems to break due to a change in our code.

Maintaining backward compatibility doesn't come without challenges. It increases the complexity of the module because the API needs to understand not just a single type of request but multiple types. Our code may need to handle missing information (which may have been introduced in version 2 of the API) or different information (such as changes to the list of enumerated strings in version 2), and so on.

If you cannot maintain backward compatibility with an old version, be sure you notify your clients well in advance, allowing them enough time to make the necessary changes. In public APIs, I've encountered cases where we notified our customers a year and a half before deprecating the API!

Forward compatibility is also important, depending on how we deploy our software. Some companies deploy software in release trains, where all modules are deployed once a week. Due to the challenges of defining the correct order for weekly module deployment, modules are deployed in a predetermined sequence. A client already using the new version 2 of the API may be deployed before the module that supports version 2. For a few seconds (or minutes or hours, depending on the duration and complexity of the deployment), clients may be making API calls using version 2 while the module still only understands version 1.

In such situations, you should ensure not only backward compatibility but also forward compatibility. This means your modules should be able to handle requests gracefully, even if they are in formats that the modules do not yet understand.

7.2.3   *Provide clean extension points*

Modules should offer clean ways for other modules to extend their functionality, especially when a module's behavior needs constant changes, evolution, or customization for other modules. By providing extension points, teams can avoid the need for frequent synchronization whenever they require minor changes in the module's behavior. For example, consider the delivery team modifying the Delivery module whenever the store sells a new item. Such an approach doesn't scale well.

I once worked with a team that developed billing systems for a company offering various software-as-a-service products. Each time a new product was introduced, we had to adjust to support the company's payment collection method. This caused significant delays in delivering the new products. To address this, we created a new API that offered product teams a lot of flexibility. Whether they wanted to charge customers with one-off payments or a combination of one-off and recurring monthly payments, they could do it easily using the new API. As a result, teams could release new products without needing to involve us, and we were pleased to no longer receive emergency requests with unreasonable deadlines every month.

We discussed designing flexible classes in chapter 5, and the same principles apply at the module level. In essence, flexibility in modules can range from offering simple interfaces that other modules implement to fully flexible APIs, allowing clients to make complex requests as needed.

7.2.4   *Code as if your module will be used by someone with different needs*

It is essential for modules to be as decoupled from each other as possible. One helpful approach to consider is coding your module as if it were to be used by another company. The only way a module can be designed to work for another company is by avoiding coupling it to the specific decisions of your current company.

You may think this is a waste of time. It is crucial to carefully reason what needs to be decoupled and not abstract everything arbitrarily. As discussed in previous chapters, you must find the right places to abstract and create extension points. But 5 or 10 years from now, your module will probably be used by another company. Why? Because your company today will not be the same in 5 or 10 years. Companies change, evolve, and grow; the code must adapt accordingly. The most cost-effective way to allow this growth is by designing modules that support such changes.

Many companies make the mistake of creating in-house frameworks driven by the desire to precisely match their current work methods and needs. They forget that work methods will change in a few years, and without investing in flexibility beforehand, refactoring the entire codebase to accommodate those changes will be much more expensive.

For example, suppose a module requires all other modules to register before using a feature. A future-proof approach would be for this module to offer a Register API that other modules can use to register themselves. A less future-proof method would be to have a hardcoded array listing other modules, requiring changes whenever a new module emerges.

7.2.5 *Modules should have clear ownership and engagement rules*

Focusing on designing good modules from a technical perspective isn't enough in large modularized systems. We also need rules to help teams know who to talk to and how to communicate in case of problems. That's why modules should have clear ownership and engagement rules.

By *ownership*, I mean it has to be evident to every team in the organization who's responsible for the module (see figure 7.2). For example, if there's a bug, who fixes it? If maintenance or evolution needs to be performed, who does it? Deciding who owns what may be a trivial problem in small-scale software development, but it becomes a significant challenge as the company grows. The problems arising from lack of ownership are numerous. The lack of clear ownership leads to the disappearance of knowledge about the module over time; no engineers feel responsible for improving its design, developers are never confident about changing it, and the number of bugs starts to increase, among other problems.

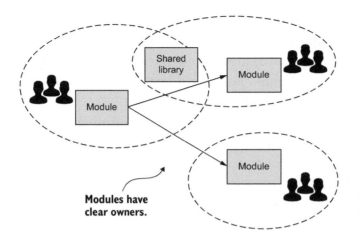

Modules have clear owners.

Figure 7.2   Modules should have clear ownership.

Defining engagement rules is also essential when different teams develop dozens of modules. If I identify a bug in a module that doesn't belong to me, can I fix it, or should I open a request? Does it require code review from at least one code owner, or is it enough that the continuous integration pipeline passes?

I won't discuss which approach is better because that's getting closer to the social aspects rather than the technical aspects of object-oriented design, but these things must be clearly defined. A great book on the social/technical challenges of building performant autonomous teams is *Team Topologies* by Matthew Skelton and Manuel Pais (IT Revolution, 2019). I strongly recommend that everyone read it.

Team topologies in a nutshell

In a nutshell, *Team Topologies* proposes four fundamental team topologies and three ways of interaction. The four topologies are as follows:

- *Stream-aligned teams* focused on a segment of the business domain
- *Enabling teams* to help stream-aligned teams overcome obstacles
- *Complicated subsystem teams* dedicated to overly complex systems that require specific expertise
- *Platform teams* to accelerate the delivery of stream-aligned teams by providing internal products

And these are the three ways these different teams can collaborate:

- *Collaboration*—Teams work together for a specific amount of time to explore new things or solve a new problem.
- *X-as-a-service*—One team provides and one team consumes something "as a service."
- *Facilitation*—One team helps and mentors another team.

As the book discusses, explicitly designing the teams' goals, ownership boundaries, and interaction modes is critical to accelerate and increase productivity.

7.3 *No intimacy between modules*

Modules should aim to minimize their level of interdependence with other modules. The less they know about each other, the better. Modules shouldn't allow others to inspect their internal workings too extensively. This practice ensures that modules can evolve gracefully without causing disruptions in other parts of the system.

In object-oriented design, having too much knowledge about the internal details of other code components is frowned on, and the same applies at the module level. Modules that are overly aware of how other modules function are more susceptible to breaking if those other modules undergo changes in their internal implementation.

For example, consider a module that uses caching to improve response times. No other module should have to care or be aware of this caching process. By enforcing this rule, the original module can modify its caching mechanism without fear of breaking other modules that rely on it.

All the principles of encapsulation and information hiding we discussed earlier are equally relevant here. Now, let's focus on ideas that emerge when thinking at the module level.

7.3.1 *Make modules and clients responsible for the lack of intimacy*

Ensuring that modules remain unaware of the internal details of other modules is a responsibility shared between the module and its clients. In an ideal world, clients wouldn't have to worry about this because modules would be perfectly designed, and no details would ever leak. But in reality, our designs are often imperfect, and due to a combination of limited knowledge (about what the application needs to do, not lack of design knowledge) and time pressure, we sometimes make suboptimal decisions.

These less-than-ideal decisions may become apparent to clients. Just because a module leaks information doesn't mean clients must use it. Instead, clients should ignore the information and hope the module will be fixed one day without causing any negative effects.

If another team develops the leaking module, it's a kind gesture to drop that team a message and try to understand why it's happening. There might be a valid reason, or it could be an oversight, and your message could serve as a helpful refactoring suggestion.

7.3.2   *Don't depend on internal classes*

In monoliths, it's common for all modules to be in the same code-base, and all a developer needs to do to access classes from another module is to declare them in the package manager. This grants development teams great power because it requires zero effort to start using a new module. However, it also places a significant responsibility on them to ensure that they don't use classes that are meant to be internal to a specific module, as shown in figure 7.3.

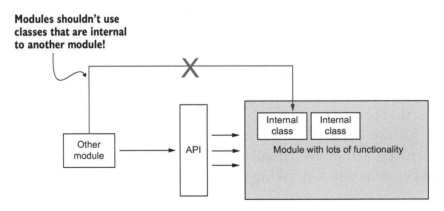

Figure 7.3   Modules shouldn't use internal classes of other modules.

Modules coupling themselves to the internal implementation of other modules is a recipe for disaster. If an internal class changes, this may break the modules coupled to it. Also, when the team learns that other modules are coupled with internal details of their module, they will refrain from changing them because they don't want to break others. This may hinder their ability to keep improving their code.

I remember watching a talk by Marc Philipp (https://github .com/marcphilipp), one of the lead developers of JUnit 5, the most popular Java testing framework. He mentioned that it was too hard to make changes in JUnit 4, as any change could break clients, including famous IDEs like Eclipse. He gave the audience a remarkable example: some IDEs were coupled to the field names of internal classes. This meant an IDE could stop working if developers renamed a field. This clearly illustrates how bad coupling to internal details is for everyone.

Teams can help other teams avoid making this mistake in a few ways. The first is to document the module's API thoroughly. It should be clear to other developers what they can use from that module. Some software designers make it explicit that all classes other modules can use are in a `public` or `api` package, and no other class should be used.

Teams can also put tools in place to enforce these rules. For instance, ArchUnit is a well-known Java framework that allows developers to declare architectural constraints. If a module starts depending on a class from a forbidden package, the tool will alert the developers. The Java Platform Modules System (JPMS) also helps developers by preventing code compilation if they use something they shouldn't.

Depending on an internal class tends to occur when a module needs a functionality already implemented by another module but not exposed as a public API. Reusing entities is another common cause of such coupling. For example, if another module implements an `Invoice` class, it may be tempting to reuse it instead of reimplementing it.

This reuse seems logical and more efficient than reimplementing it, but what if the other team changes that class in a way you don't expect or want? Remember that the two teams are likely separated for a reason. They may have different stakeholders and different perspectives on the business. They may change Invoice in a way that makes sense to them but not you.

If you find yourself in such a situation, stop and think: Can you make the functionality into something that other modules can use? Can you transform it into an API? Should you create a new small module to hold this new feature so that it becomes a standard library between both teams and you share the responsibility to keep it compatible?

If the answer to these questions is no, how bad would it be to duplicate the functionality? Duplication can be problematic, but having to synchronize teams every time a class changes may cost you even more.

7.3.3 *Monitor the web of dependencies*

Monitoring the web of dependencies and how it grows is vital, especially in large-scale systems with dozens or hundreds of modules. Before you know it, you may have modules coupled with others in ways you don't want, becoming so intertwined that refactoring becomes virtually impossible.

Besides the maintenance cost, where changes in one module may affect another, complex dependency trees can result in longer build times. It's not uncommon to see companies with build times exceeding an hour, mainly because the compiler struggles to recompile a large amount of code whenever a highly used module in the system is altered. Although build systems like Bazel have improved over time and become smarter about what to recompile, it's best to address this problem at the root by preventing the dependency tree from growing wildly in the first place.

Modules that offer a clear API and are designed with flexibility and extensibility in mind—meaning modules that follow the principles discussed in this book—tend to be less problematic. Changes in their internals don't trigger breaking changes or force other modules to recompile. However, we know that reality isn't always ideal, and large software systems inevitably have modules that were not well designed from the beginning. These modules require careful monitoring.

In my experience, the primary reason for wild growth of coupling is that modules start depending on other, poorly designed modules because they need one little thing another module offers. My suggestion is the same as in the previous section: search for opportunities not to depend on these large modules. Can you extract this functionality to another module or at least expose it to clients in a less coupled and more elegant way? Note that there's no clear answer or silver bullet for this problem, and you also don't want to end up with a million tiny modules with a single class each. You have to explore, try, monitor, and improve.

7.3.4   Monoliths or microservices?

I've refrained from discussing whether modules should all live in a monolith or multiple individual microservices. There are great books on this topic—especially the two authored by Sam Newman, *Building Microservices, Second Edition,* and *Monoliths to Microservices* (O'Reilly, 2021 and 2019, respectively)—so I won't delve too deeply into it.

All the principles discussed in this chapter apply to both approaches. It doesn't matter whether it's a monolith or a microservice; you don't want it to become too intimate, neglect backward compatibility, or offer a complex API. Each approach has its challenges. Although it's much easier to apply the "extract functionality to a module" principle in a monolith than in a microservices world, it's also much easier to become too intimate with another module in a monolith world. Ultimately, you must pick your favorite approach and fight against the growth of its complexity.

7.3.5   Consider events as a way to decouple modules

Event-based architectures have become popular in recent years due to their remarkable way of decoupling modules and services. The idea is that instead of coupling modules with each other through calls, we publish an event announcing what just happened, and interested modules subscribe to this stream of events.

For example, let's say the Billing service makes an explicit call to the Delivery service whenever an invoice is marked as paid. This strongly couples Delivery with Billing. If Delivery changes how it receives this paid notification, Billing may also have to change.

In an event-driven architecture, Billing publishes an InvoicePaid event. The services interested in this event, such as Delivery, subscribe to the stream, and whenever a new event pops up, they get the event and do their jobs. Note that Billing is no longer coupled to Delivery. Billing has no idea who listens to these events. Delivery can change as much as it wants, and Billing won't be affected. Even new services can start listening to this event without requiring the billing team.

As with any architectural decision, event-driven architecture design is full of trade-offs. On the plus side, in addition to decoupling modules, it's easier to listen and react to events than to provide APIs for every single action you need in your system. We have lots of good architectural patterns and infrastructure to support this. On the negative side, it can quickly become hard to see all the events raised in the system. Monitoring also becomes trickier because following events requires more work than following a sequence of method calls. Backward compatibility is still important, because if the billing team changes the event's content, it may affect listening modules. If you are curious about event-driven architectures, read *Building Event-Driven Microservices: Using Organizational Data at Scale* by Adam Bellemare (O'Reilly, 2020) or *Microservices Patterns* by Chris Richardson (Manning, 2018).

7.3.6 *Example: The notification system*

Notifying participants about the training courses they're enrolled in became core to PeopleGrow! These notifications could be sent through email, direct messages, or WhatsApp. The logic around it grew too much, prompting the company to decide it was time to move notifications to another module and allocate them to a dedicated development team.

The assembled team decided to implement Notification (the new module's name) as a separate service. That would allow them to have a different release cycle and set up different service-level objectives (SLOs). The team drafted the first responsibilities of this new service:

- Sending notifications through different channels
- Supporting different notification templates and messages that can be customized by clients of the service

The team decided that the service should be offered via a web API and should be accessible through a collection of endpoints. JSON was chosen as the format for communication.

In their first modeling session, the team focused on designing the core of their service: how clients should request a notification to be sent. They decided that the service must offer three different APIs to get started:

- The first offers clients a way to create a new notification. Say they want to notify participants who enroll in a specific training course. This API should then be created to create the notification. The API requires the message, the supported media (only email? email and chat?) and when it should be sent (now, *X* days later, *X* days before the course starts, and so on).
- The second offers clients a way to add the list of participants to the notification. Clients should pass the ID of the notification (returned by the previous API) and the list of emails. The client can call this API as often as they want with new participants.
- The third offers clients a way to remove participants from a specific notification.

The following listing shows an interface that can represent this API. The team worked hard to ensure that this interface is simple yet powerful, as we discussed in this chapter. The interface offers three methods, one for each of the actions described. `Medium` and `Dispatch-Time` are enumerations that give users a specific list of options.

Listing 7.1   Notification API

```
interface NotificationAPI {                    ◁──┐ Interface with the three operations
    Notification createNotification(                 offered by the Notification API
       String message,
       List<Medium> supportedMedium,
       List<DispatchTime> times);
    void addParticipant(int notificationId, String participantEmail);
    void removeParticipant(int notificationId, String participantEmail);
}
```

```
enum Medium {        ◁——— Three types of supported media
    EMAIL,
    CHAT,
    WHATSAPP;
}
enum DispatchTime {        ◁——— Four types of supported dispatch times
    RIGHT_NOW,
    ONE_WEEK_BEFORE,
    DAY_BEFORE,
    ONE_HOUR_BEFORE;
}
```

To support backward compatibility (another important topic discussed in this chapter), the team clarified that they can always add more items to the `Medium` and `DispatchTime` enumerators but can't remove any of them. The same is true for the `Notification` structure that's returned to the clients whenever they create a new notification: fields can be added but not removed, nor can their semantics be changed.

Behind the scenes, the team decided the API would be implemented in Java, with Spring Boot as the framework and Postgres as the database. Asynchronous jobs poll the database for the next notifications to be sent. The team considered introducing a queue like RabbitMQ but decided that could be done later. The API doesn't let internal details leak (another principle from this chapter), so this refactoring can eventually be done without breaking the clients.

> ## Security concerns
> When designing such an API in a real-world system, you have to take care of authentication and authorization so only users with the proper permissions can make calls to the API. Security goes beyond the scope of this book, but it's interesting to think about whether such security aspects would have to be reflected in the design of the API. I'll leave this as an exercise for you.

7.4 Exercises

Think through the following questions or discuss them with a colleague:

1 Have you ever worked on a microservices or monolithic project with multiple modules? What were the primary challenges related to how they were designed to work together?

2 In the project you are currently working on, how intimate are the modules? What should you do to reduce such intimacy?

3 Have you ever encountered a problem due to poor backward compatibility? What caused it? What did you do to avoid going through the same problem again?

4 What other practices does your company have around ensuring that modules (or services) work well together?

Summary

- Modules should provide simple interfaces on top of complex features.

- A good module doesn't force clients to change whenever its internal details change.

- Modules should provide clear communication interfaces that are stable and backward compatible. If flexibility is needed, modules should offer easy-to-use extension points.

- Don't let modules know about each other's details. Modules should do their best to hide their details, and clients should do their best not to be coupled to any leaked details.

- Modules should have clear ownership and engagement rules to simplify communication among the different teams working on different modules.

Being pragmatic

8

This chapter covers
- Why being pragmatic matters
- Why you should never stop refactoring
- Why you should never stop learning about object-oriented design

Congratulations! You've finished this journey through the six most important characteristics of simple object-oriented design:

- Small units of code
- Consistent objects
- Proper dependency management
- Good abstractions
- Properly handled infrastructure
- Well modularized

In this chapter, I discuss a few pieces of advice that I also consider essential to keep object-oriented designs as simple as possible.

Some were briefly mentioned in previous chapters but are so important that I've dedicated a separate section to them.

8.1 *Be pragmatic and go only as far as you must*

It's easy to get stuck in an infinite loop of design improvements, especially for engineers who appreciate a well-designed system. Even simple design decisions can branch out into numerous possibilities.

Striving for the best possible design is essential for a highly maintainable, simple object-oriented system. But it's important to remember that our primary goal is not to write beautiful designs but rather to deliver functional software as efficiently as possible. A good design enables that goal, but it's not the end. Finding the right tradeoff between exploring the perfect design and settling for a good-enough design is a challenging task that improves with experience over time.

8.2 *Refactor aggressively but in small steps*

Never stop refactoring. Refactoring is the most effective tool to combat the growth of complexity. The more frequently you refactor, the cheaper and quicker it becomes because you have less code to refactor, and your skills will improve.

Engineers who are less enthusiastic about constant refactoring may argue that it wastes time. They may ask, "Why should I rename this variable? It makes no difference," or say "This is nitpicking!" But once you realize that refactoring is an investment with significant returns, you'll find it easier to embrace.

As we discussed earlier, pragmatism is essential. Don't overdo it. You don't need to refactor every bit of functionality that is easy to maintain. You may not need to refactor—at least urgently—pieces of code that never change or have proven themselves in production. Pay attention to the signals, listen to your code, and refactor when necessary.

8.3 *Accept that your code won't ever be perfect*

Life as an engineer becomes much easier when you realize that your code, design, and architecture will never be perfect. Do your best with the information and resources available at a given moment. As you learn more about the system, you may discover better possibilities.

As I've mentioned, your code doesn't have to be perfect. "Good enough," as discussed in the previous chapters, is sufficient in most cases. But you should never stop writing better code every day.

8.4   Consider redesigns

Don't dismiss the possibility of redesigns, especially in the early stages of development when refactoring is still cost effective. I understand the need for pragmatism. Redesigning and reimplementing something can be costly. But if you can see that the current approach is leading you to a dead end, it's best to refactor it as soon as possible.

I've encountered codebases where developers talked for years about redesigning parts of the system but never found the time to do it. Consequently, the codebase turned into a tangled mess. If you wait until the code becomes unbearable, you may reach a point where refactoring is no longer feasible.

John Osterhout's book, *A Philosophy of Software Design*, states that he makes the best design decisions on the third attempt at designing something. In other words, it takes him two versions to understand what the design should look like. So as soon as you realize there's a better way to do something, start planning the refactoring.

8.5   You owe this to junior developers

I've met talented developers who spent their early years in companies that didn't prioritize code quality. As a result, these developers faced challenges in upskilling themselves when they moved on to other jobs.

Novice developers learn a lot from the code they work on and the engineers they are surrounded by. It's our responsibility to help the newer generations understand the importance of good code. We achieve this by setting an example, constantly working to reduce complexity in our code, and continually seeking ways to improve the design of our systems.

8.6   *References*

There are many books about object-oriented design, and I've learned a lot from them. I strongly recommend you read other perspectives on this topic:

- *Domain Language: Tackling Complexity in the Heart of Software* by Eric Evans (Addison- Wesley, 2003)
- *Implementing Domain Driven Design* by Vaughn Vernon (Addison-Wesley, 2-13)
- *A Philosophy of Software Design* by John Ousterhout (Yaknyam Press, 2021)
- *Head First Design Patterns: Building Extensible and Maintainable Object-Oriented Software, 2nd ed.*, by Eric Freeman and Elisabeth Robson (O'Reilly, 2021)
- *Building Maintainable Software, Ten Guidelines for Future-Proof Code* by Joost Visser et al. (www.softwareimprovementgroup.com/ publications/ebook-building-maintainable-software)
- *Refactoring to Patterns* by Joshua Kerievsky (www.industriallogic .com/xp/refactoring)
- *Object Design Style Guide, from Python to PHP* by Matthias Noback (https://matthiasnoback.nl/book/style-guide-for-object-design)
- *Refactoring: Improving the Design of Existing Code* by Martin Fowler (https://martinfowler.com/books/refactoring.html)
- *Object-Oriented Analysis and Design with Applications, 3rd ed.*, by Grady Booch et al. (Addison-Wesley, 2007)
- *Growing Object-Oriented Software, Guided by Tests* by Steve Freeman and Nat Pryce (Addison-Wesley, 2009)

These are the books that affected me, but there are many others. Never stop learning about object-oriented design!

8.7   *Exercises*

Think through the following questions or discuss them with a colleague:

1 How often do you refactor your design? Are you a refactoring addict, or is refactoring something you only do when it's really needed?

2 Being pragmatic isn't easy. How do you decide when to go for a more elegant design solution?

3 People say, "There's nothing more permanent than a temporary workaround." How often have you seen a workaround become permanent in the codebase? Why do you think that happened? Is there something you can do to avoid it?

4 Have you ever redesigned (parts of) a software system? What challenges did you face? Did you benefit from it in the end?

Summary

- Designing object-oriented systems is a fine art that requires mastering.
- Complexity tends to grow in any software system. It's your job to keep fighting against this growth. It costs less if done every day.
- A simple object-oriented system keeps its code simple, objects consistent, and dependencies adequately managed; it has good abstractions, handles infrastructure code properly, and is well modularized.
- Strive for the perfect design, but know that it doesn't exist. Good-enough designs are often what you need.
- This book shows my take on simple object-oriented design after 20 years of building good and bad software systems. There are many other good books on this topic, read some of them and form your own opinions about what constitutes a good design.

index

A new online reading experience

liveBook, our online reading platform, adds a new dimension to your Manning books, with features that make reading, learning, and sharing easier than ever. A liveBook version of your book is included FREE with every Manning book.

This next generation book platform is more than an online reader. It's packed with unique features to upgrade and enhance your learning experience.

- Add your own notes and bookmarks
- One-click code copy
- Learn from other readers in the discussion forum
- Audio recordings and interactive exercises
- Read all your purchased Manning content in any browser, anytime, anywhere

As an added bonus, you can search every Manning book and video in liveBook—even ones you don't yet own. Open any liveBook, and you'll be able to browse the content and read anything you like.*

Find out more at www.manning.com/livebook-program.

Open reading is limited to 10 minutes per book daily